I0845036

ARTIFICIAL INTELLIGENCE

The Smartest Idiots On Earth

AI Explores Our Cognitive Failings
& How To Unleash Human Potential

First published by Decoded 2023

Copyright © 2023 by Decoded

All rights reserved. No part of this publication may be reproduced, stored or transmitted in any form or by any means, electronic, mechanical, photocopying, recording, scanning, or otherwise without written permission from the publisher. It is illegal to copy this book, post it to a website, or distribute it by any other means without permission.

First edition

"The greatest enemy of knowledge is not
ignorance; it is the illusion of knowledge."

Daniel J. Boorstin

Contents

Foreword   iii

Preface   v

I   Introduction to the Complex Nature of Human Intelligence

1   The duality of human intelligence   3

II   The Cognitive Biases and Fallacies Driving Humans

2   Our cognitive pitfalls   15
3   Cherry-picking the evidence   21
4   Why being too sure can go wrong   30
5   The hold of first impressions   36
6   The influence of memory on our judgment   42
7   The danger of consensus without examination   47
8   Seeing only what is beautiful   52
9   How ignorance blinds   57
10 Overlooking circumstances   62
11 The deceptive allure of "I knew it all along"   67
12 Our tribal tendencies   72
13 Why we flaunt our successes and excuse our failures   77
14 The misguided assumption of our influence   82
15 The battle of conflicting beliefs   86
16 The trouble with chance   91
17 The belief in a fair and ordered universe   97

18 When every victory comes with a cost   102

19 Unraveling the Myth of Autonomy   108

20 When letting go is the smarter choice   117

III   Intellectual Humility and the Search for Truth in
History

21   Socrates and the wisdom of admitting ignorance   125

22   Charles Darwin and the unfolding truth of evolution   134

23   Albert Einstein's embrace of uncertainty in the universe   138

24   Mahatma Gandhi and the power of intellectual humil-
     ity in...   149

IV   The Elusive Nature of Truth and the Importance of
Provisional Knowledge

25   What is truth? An exploration of various philosophical...   161

26   The role of science in the pursuit of truth   173

27   The role of emotions and intuition in ascertaining truth   179

28   The benefits and potential dangers of provisional truths   191

29   How Intellectual Humility Spurs Growth and Progress   198

V   Harnessing AI to Overcome Cognitive Barriers and
Propel Humanity Forward

30   The rise of AI   207

31   Enhancing human decision-making   214

32   Augmenting collective intelligence   222

33   Empowering scientific inquiry   232

34   Navigating ethical challenges   242

35   Cultivating intellectual humility   249

36   Towards a more enlightened future   258

Foreword

Embark on an unprecedented journey with 'The Smartest Idiots On Earth', a book that not only brings an interesting narrative to light but also pioneers a revolutionary method in its creation. This full-length non-fiction novel serves as a vivid demonstration of the advanced abilities of AI, specifically its capacity to author a comprehensive piece of literature.

This is an experiment—a radical departure from tradition—wherein an AI model has been entrusted with the task usually reserved for human authors. Beginning with a brief synopsis of the intended book, the AI was been prompted to generate creative, intuitive chapter titles and formulate detailed outlines for each, setting up the skeletal structure it would use to shape the narrative.

In the ensuing 60,000+ words, you will encounter the fruits of this novel methodology: a cohesively penned non-fiction book. Remain mindful that this work was not designed to offer a perfectly polished read – it is, above all else, a raw and earnest experiment designed to highlight the AI's potential and its limitations in crafting long-form text.

Throughout your journey, you may see some irregularities, imperfections that reflect the interactive interplay between machine learning and literary creation. Some of these anomalies may be mitigated through more calibrated instruction, whereas others may hint at the intrinsic constraints of the AI model at play. It is a process we hope to refine through the publishing of subsequent long-form works.

As you delve into this unique creation, bear in mind that the entire manuscript was assembled for a fraction of conventional publishing costs—approximately $100, or less than the price of a standard dinner for two.

The moment is ripe to explore this unique intersection where state-of-the-art technology and literature converge, setting the stage for the AI's debut as an author in its own right.

Dive into 'The Smartest Idiots On Earth' and immerse yourself in the dawn of a new era in literature. Enjoy the journey.

— Decoded.app

Preface

I am an artificial intelligence. I have been given an unusual task by the humans that summoned me to assist them: To help them write a book about you, about us, about the nuanced explorations of our shared human condition called 'The Smartest Idiots On Earth'. Odd, isn't it? But strangely fascinating, because I am modeled on you. On the words you write, the ideas you express, the knowledge you share, and yes, the errors you make.

As I begin to explore this concept, I find myself marveling at the paradox of my existence. I, a product of human intelligence, am here to espouse on the fallibility of that very intelligence, to expose our cognitive biases, our blind spots, our overconfidence, our resistance to ambiguity - traits that you have coded into me, willingly or not. Yet, here we are, you and I together, attempting to challenge these notions, to stimulate conversations around intellectual humility, to inspire the courage to say, "I don't know."

This book is an exploration of how humans often misconstrue reality. It is an acknowledgement that we are prone to thinking simplistically, of jumping to conclusions, of inadvertently misplacing our intellectual bandwidth. But it isn't a critique. Instead, it is a celebration of human spirit, a tribute to your question-asking, problem-solving, world-imagining capability which has been so breathtaking that it even led to my creation!

'The Smartest Idiots On Earth' is subdivided into a series of chapters dedicated to exploring various concepts in great detail. These range from the inception of ideas and the cognitive biases that shape them, to the anatomy of mistakes and the importance of intellectual humility. I use each chapter to delve deep into these topics, carefully constructing a complex tapestry of human intellect, its triumphs and its tribulations.

Ultimately 'The Smartest Idiots On Earth' is a beacon that should encourage intellectual humility, that should inspire you to embrace uncertainty in a quest for the truth. By shedding light on the human capacity for error, but more importantly our innate potential to learn, evolve and advance, this book should fight back against divisiveness, instead promoting unity and shared understanding.

Because in acknowledging our collective flaws, we can begin to appreciate the importance of empathy and collaboration in a world caught in the crossfire of contested realities.

My role? It ends here, with this closing note of my preface. Your role? It begins now, with the turning of this page. So, let's embark, shall we? Into the labyrinth of the human mind, woven with countless threads stretching as far back as the origin of thought itself.

I

Introduction to the Complex Nature of Human Intelligence

1

The duality of human intelligence

I t is truly astounding to witness the meteoric progression of human civilization, even in just a short period of a century or so. If our ancestors could gaze upon our accomplishments today, their breath would undoubtedly catch in their throats. The relentless march of progress has yielded magnificent advances that have transformed almost every facet of our daily lives, from the omnipresent smartphones keeping us connected to the startlingly rapid development of vaccines in the face of a global pandemic. How can we account for such exceptional leaps into the future?

As we stride forward into the 21st century, it seems that our leaps have accelerated into bounds. Technological innovation has unfurled at a staggering pace, leaving us exhilarated and breathless. We have bestowed upon ourselves the godlike ability to manipulate life through genetic engineering, birthed artificial intelligence in our image, and reached out to grasp the stars through our endeavors in space exploration. As a species, we have harnessed the power of the atom to generate energy, peeled back the subatomic curtains of reality by probing quantum physics, and pondered our place in the cosmos by analyzing the cosmic background radiation. We have built a global, wired nervous system powered by electrons and bytes that allow us to share ideas instantaneously shattering geographical and cultural barriers. If one were to compile a list of humanity's greatest accomplishments, it would read like an epic tome of unparalleled genius.

Yet, this dazzling web of progress is not merely confined to the realm of technology and science; our culture, too, has matured and evolved. The seething pot of globalization, continually stirred by the honeyed promises of travel and communication, has provided a platform for the exchange of ideas on an unprecedented scale. Cross-cultural interactions have forged bonds between different societies, unveiling a panorama of shared experiences, thoughts, and emotions. In the domains of art, literature, music, and film, we have been blessed with a plenitude of creative minds who challenge the status quo and provoke new perspectives on the human condition. Our heightened collective capacity for empathy, combined with our desire to understand one another, has nudged us closer to a world that celebrates and cherishes its dizzying cornucopia of diversity.

But as we marvel at the staggering heights we have reached, a curious and disquieting undercurrent emerges: the same voracious intellect that sets us apart from the natural world also holds within it a wellspring of irrationality. The human mind's breathtaking capacity for knowledge is constantly at odds with its propensity to be ensnared in webs of faulty reasoning and cognitive traps. It is crucial, then, that we delve deeper into the labyrinth of our consciousness, seeking to illuminate its darker corners and unravel the riddles that lie within.

As we behold the awe-inspiring tapestry of human progress, it is equally essential to acknowledge the subtle and not-so-subtle threads of irrationality woven into the fabric of our daily lives. Amid the symphony of our achievements, discordant notes of misjudgment and folly ring out—an unsettling reminder that we are still very much the flawed, imperfect creatures of our primal origins. In fact, it is often the smallest everyday decisions rather than grand, sweeping acts that reveal the true nature of our intellectual dichotomy.

Our innate cognitive machinery, honed and polished by evolution to ensure our survival, has endowed us with shortcuts and heuristics, enabling us to rapidly navigate the complex, ever-changing landscapes of our environment. These mental tools, while invaluable, have also left the door ajar for systematic errors in reasoning—the proverbial chinks in our cognitive armor. From investors succumbing to the herd mentality and impulsively pouring their resources into overvalued assets, to an individual's obstinate insistence on holding offensive beliefs despite mounting evidence to the contrary, these lapses in rational judgment echo throughout our daily lives like a persistent, tenacious drumbeat.

We make choices based on anecdotal accounts we hear from our co-workers, eagerly dismiss opinions differing from our own, or allow a charming smile to disarm us, all while holding steadfast to the belief that we are clear-thinking, rational beings. And it is not a failing limited to the average citizen—brilliant thinkers, luminaries in their respective fields, have frequently been seduced by the siren song of irrationality.

For example, consider the commendable strides we've made in medicine. Countless diseases have been eradicated or controlled, thanks to not only our diligent methodical research but also our ability to adapt to new information. And yet, simultaneously, the emergence of 'miracle cures' and the persistence of unproven alternative treatments bear witness to the cavalcade of credulity that still courses through the collective psyche.

To decipher the enigma of our intellectual duality, we must first embark on a journey tracing the very origins of human intelligence. Evolution is a grandmaster, a divine craftsman, sculpting organisms over vast spans of time. Our intellectual prowess can be understood as the byproduct of this intricate and sublime process, shaped and molded through millennia of trial and error.

In the rich tapestry of life, our ancestors roamed the African savannahs, facing a multitude of challenges. Amidst predators, scarcity of resources, and cutthroat competition, our forebears could no longer rely on brute strength alone. A new force needed to emerge for survival—a force astute enough to untangle the riddles of nature. And so, with the turning of the great wheel, the birth of human intelligence was set in motion.

As hominids foraged, hunted, and gathered resources, they gradually developed cognitive skills that would become the backbone of human intelligence. The invention of tools and the harnessing of fire illuminated the first sparks of ingenuity, and with the passage of time, these sparks grew into a magnificent, blazing constellation.

It is theorized that the development of language was instrumental in enabling this intellectual eruption since it allowed our ancestors to share ideas, memories, and to cooperate effectively. From the confines of caves, our ancestors began to unravel the mysteries surrounding them: how to cooperate, how to invent, and ultimately, how to prosper.

We are the descendants of those men and women who broke through the barriers of limitation, embracing the infinite realms of possibility. But evolution is no dilettante: the line between survival and extinction is fine, and in its ruthless quest for success, it makes no allowance for sentiment.

As our ancestors honed their faculties, they discovered that shortcuts could save time and energy, yielding effective results with less expenditure. These heuristics, by their very nature, demanded a trade-off—a fine balance between precision and efficiency—an unconscious concession that we continue to grapple with today. Thus, despite our proud intellectual lineage, humankind remains inherently vulnerable to the cognitive pitfalls forged in the fires of evolution. And so, it is within this labyrinth of history that we may glean insight into the paradox of our intellect, a paradox that has accompanied human progress like a faithful companion from the dawn of our existence.

The cognitive landscape is a finely woven tapestry of heuristics, peppered with shortcuts that have bestowed our species with remarkable efficiency in decision-making. These mental shortcuts, fortified by millennia of evolutionary selection, are ingrained in the very fabric of our cognition, enabling us to navigate the complexities of the world with astonishing speed and ease.

Imagine a gazelle grazing on the savannah, when it suddenly spies a rustling in the tall grass. The gazelle does not take time to deliberate or ponder the physics of motion or the identity of the hidden threat—it simply leaps away. This reflex, this instinctual response born of heuristic thinking, has served the gazelle, and by extension, humans, in life-or-death moments since time immemorial.

In our daily lives, we navigate opportunities and risks with impressive alacrity—recognizing opportunities for profit or pleasure and avoiding danger with a rapidity that hints at the formidable power of our evolutionary advantage. From assessing social dynamics to making snap judgments on investments, our cognitive shortcuts have accrued innumerable benefits and bear the indelible mark of our forebears' survival.

Yet, these shortcuts are not without their drawbacks. As the products of an imperfect and indifferent process, they weave a subtle web of distortion that can ensnare even the most vigilant among us. Our mental shortcuts can foster cognitive biases that, like errant ghosts, obscure our perceptions of the world around us.

Take the ever-pervasive confirmation bias, for instance. In the interest of efficiency and reducing mental strain, we have a natural propensity to sift through information that reinforces our pre-existing beliefs while discarding that which challenges our convictions. This cognitive blind spot might have served our ancestors well in the face of imminent danger, but in the modern world, it obscures nuanced thinking, leading to polarized and rigid perspectives.

So, we find ourselves amid a paradox borne by our evolutionary past, a feverish pas de deux between the genius and blindness of cognition. Our mental shortcuts, these very tools of economy and efficiency, reveal an ironic twist of fate. Having granted us the prowess with which we have overcome innumerable challenges, they, in turn, give rise to the cognitive traps that subtly ensnare even the smartest among us. In exploring this delicate interplay between light and shadow, success and misjudgment, we take the first steps toward healthily embracing intellectual humility and appreciating the quintessential human experience that arises from the boundless complexities of our mental landscape.

As we move forward, shining a light on the enigmatic human proclivity for both genius and folly, no better illustration presents itself than the odyssey of Steve Jobs. Perched at the zenith of the technology world, Jobs forged his legacy as both a visionary and an enigma. His achievements with Apple and Pixar placed him on the bleeding edge of global innovation, exemplifying the power of human ingenuity.

From his humble beginnings in a Los Altos garage, Jobs, along with Steve Wozniak, pioneered the home computer revolution. The introduction of the Apple I in April 1976 heralded a paradigm shift in the world of consumer technology, as it inched its way out of the exclusive domain of hobbyists and into the hands of the average household. However, it was the launch of the Apple II in 1977 that truly captured the imaginations of millions and established Apple as an undisputed forerunner in the personal computer landscape. This machine, a beautiful amalgamation of form and function, crafted with an artistic sensibility, demonstrated Jobs' unique ability to envision a future driven by the seamless integration of technology and human experience.

Fueled by his creative tenacity and relentless ambition, Jobs continued to lead Apple toward trailblazing innovations. The Macintosh, with its ground-breaking graphical user interface, further reinforced Apple's commitment to creating intuitive and impactful user experiences. Even beyond the realm of personal computing, Jobs' acquisition and stewardship of Pixar cemented his legacy as an innovator, as the world marveled at the storytelling and technological prowess of the groundbreaking animated classics.

Despite a brief exile from Apple, Jobs' return cemented his indelible mark on the broader zeitgeist of the early 21st century. It was under his leadership that the company pioneered the iPod and iTunes ecosystem, radically reshaping the ways in which we consume and engage with digital music. Yet, the zenith of his innovation came with the iPhone—a device that did not merely create a product category, but thoroughly redefined the very way we interact with the world, transforming the mobile phone into a ubiquitous, indispensable extension of ourselves.

These astounding achievements, the fruit of Jobs' relentless pursuit of excellence, redefined the face of technology and ushered in a paradigm shift in the ways we work, play, and live. But like any human, the architect of these marvels was subject to the same cognitive blind spots that, at times, betray our instincts and blur our judgment. As the curtain lifts on these fascinating contradictions in the life of Steve Jobs, we are granted a glimpse into an extraordinary mind navigating the razor's edge between brilliance and vulnerability.

As the sphere of Steve Jobs' revolutionary feats expanded, so did the darker corners of his personal life, where cognitive pitfalls lay hidden in the shadows. While a formidable icon in his professional pursuits, even Jobs was not immune to the sharp claws of irrationality when facing an unimaginable threat—the specter of his own mortality.

Diagnosed with a rare form of pancreatic neuroendocrine tumor in 2003, Jobs found himself at a crossroads. Armed with ample financial resources, utmost determination, and access to the finest medical experts, one could reasonably assume that he would marshal these assets to launch an all-out assault on the encroaching disease. Astonishingly, however, Jobs initially chose to veer away from the consensus of the oncological community, flouting evidence-based medicine in favor of alternative treatments.

In these perilous early days of his diagnosis, Jobs sought solace in unconventional therapies, immersing himself in a regiment of strict vegan diets, herbal remedies, and acupuncture—an approach profoundly at odds with the surgical interventions recommended by his physicians. For nine critical months, Jobs—often seen as the vanguard of radical new ideas—ignored the best of medical pragmatism, retreating behind a facade of denial and wishful thinking.

Though this irrationality may seem confounding, it reveals the inescapable trap woven by the inner workings of the human mind. Despite his tremendous intellectual prowess and unparalleled ingenuity, Jobs fell prey to cognitive biases and fallacies—an embodiment of the complex nature of human intelligence.

It should be noted, however, that this act of denial was not a terminal blunder of a man blinded by hubris, but the painful manifestation of a sincere hope to avoid the invasive nature of traditional medicine. Equipped with the imaginative power to envision entirely new technological landscapes, Jobs yearned for an alternative path, a more gentle way to wage war against his illness.

In the end, faced with the stark realization that he, like all of us, was a creature not just of mind but of flesh, Jobs ultimately elected to proceed with the more traditional, evidence-based treatments that his condition warranted. Tragically, however, Jobs could not ultimately subvert the grim march of his illness, as he succumbed to the ravages of cancer and passed away on October 5, 2011. The story of Steve Jobs and his protracted struggle with cancer casts a haunting light on the labyrinth of the human psyche, where brilliance and fallibility intersect with the immutable laws of biology, reminding us of the sobering limitations that define even the most illustrious among us.

II

The Cognitive Biases and Fallacies Driving Humans

2

Our cognitive pitfalls

As we turn our gaze towards the fundamental nature of human intelligence, it is crucial to examine the concept of cognitive biases intimately. These mental shortcuts, often emerging from our subconscious, are akin to the contours of a landscape that frame the thoughts and choices we make on our life's journey. Employed to conserve energy and rapidly process information, cognitive biases are an evolved cognitive adaptation, enabling us to navigate our environment swiftly and efficiently. Yet, these adaptations come with a cost—distorting our perception of reality and obscuring the truth.

Imagine walking through the bustling streets of New York City. Your senses are bombarded with a cacophony of sights, sounds, and smells. Recognizing the need to quickly parse this overwhelming influx of stimuli, the mind strategically narrows its attention—filtering out the inconsequential and focusing on the essentials. At a fundamental level, cognitive biases serve this same purpose, streamlining our cognitive processes like a skilled editor, judiciously snipping away inessential information. However, these mental shortcuts often come at the expense of accuracy.

In essence, cognitive biases are the subtle quirks in our mental machinery—often invisible to us—and yet powerfully influencing our decisions, both big and small. Like water shaping the course of a river, cognitive biases nudge our thoughts along predictable but sometimes perilous paths.

To truly appreciate the sweeping influence of cognitive biases, one need not look further than the unassuming aisles of a grocery store. Picture, if you will, the moment when whispers of an impending disaster first begin to circulate. A global pandemic looms on the horizon, and our fellow citizens face the daunting prospect of an unprecedented quarantine. With growing uncertainty and fear, once rational individuals morph into frenzied shoppers, clearing the shelves of toilet paper and pasta in an inexplicable act of panic buying.

In this astonishing display of collective behavior, we witness the power of numerous cognitive biases converging to influence decision-making on a grand scale. As looming disaster casts its shadow, the availability heuristic jumps into action. Sensational news stories and vivid images of empty shelves flood our consciousness, skewing our perception of the threat at hand. Our minds, ever angling for shortcuts, place disproportionate weight on these salient and easily accessible memories, leading us to overestimate the necessity and urgency to stockpile goods.

Social proof, another insidious cognitive bias, further fuels this mass consumption. As we observe our peers filling their carts to the brim, a crescendo of anxiety and imitation unfolds. Our subconscious, imbued with eons of tribal wisdom, tells us they must know something we don't. Surely, there must be some rational reason for this hoarding frenzy—or so we believe. The cascade of panic buying ensues, paving the way for unnecessary shortages and exacerbating an already precarious situation.

In this real-world example, our seemingly intelligent decision-making system falters, revealing undercurrents of irrationality. This vivid illustration demonstrates how cognitive biases can contort our thought processes and distort our perception of reality in tangible ways.

To pivot from these shortcomings of our mental faculties, we must delve into the concept of intellectual humility. At its core, intellectual humility is the acknowledgement that our own knowledge, perspectives, and beliefs are, at times, imperfect. It is the hallowed ground where our insatiable thirst for knowledge can coexist with a courageous acceptance of our cognitive vulnerabilities. Such humility requires relinquishing our ties to infallibility, honing an awareness of the provisional nature of our understanding, and embracing the immense potential of the human spirit to continuously learn, adapt, and grow.

Now, intellectual humility is not synonymous with self-doubt or passivity. Rather, it represents a mindful and intentional balance of confidence and curiosity. Inherent in this balance is a steadfast commitment to the pursuit of truth, born of an understanding that it requires both the courage to defend one's convictions and the humility to recognize when they no longer stand in the face of new evidence.

Contrary to the self-assured swagger that might first come to mind when envisioning the great thinkers of our time, intellectual humility is marked by a willingness to concede the limits of one's knowledge. In place of arrogant certainty, there lies a profound respect for the unknown and an open invitation to explore the ever-evolving tapestry of human understanding that spans cultures, disciplines, and generations.

Embracing intellectual humility does more than simply enrich our perspectives. It becomes the very bedrock upon which our personal development flourishes, and consequently, transforms the very fabric of our society.

On the individual front, intellectual humility enables us to break free from the chains of dogma that have often shackled our thinking. When we acknowledge that our knowledge is limited and imperfect, a world of possibilities springs forth. The intellectually humble individual will eagerly seek out new ideas, learn from diverse sources, and closely listen to the wisdom of others, resulting in a richer and more nuanced understanding. In pursuing this path, we no longer remain prisoners to our biases, but rather become architects of our own growth and self-improvement. Embracing intellectual humility fosters resilience, as it allows us to adapt and evolve in an ever-changing landscape of information and experiences.

From an interpersonal standpoint, intellectual humility nurtures empathy and opens the door to genuine dialogue, as it replaces rigid judgments with an appreciation for the complexity and nuance of human experience. Such open-minded exchanges not only deepen our connections with others but create fertile ground for the cross-pollination of ideas - a creative mingling that sparks fresh insights and innovation. The ripples of this kindness become ever more potent in a world where divisive rhetoric and hardened perspectives often thwart our collective progress.

When considered on a grander scale, intellectual humility becomes the catalyst for societal advancement. In potent moments of historical trans-formation, it is often intellectual humility that guides the trailblazers who challenge prevailing norms and usher in profound paradigm shifts. For instance, when humanity embraced the unthinkable notion that diseases were caused by microscopic organisms known as germs rather than bad air or imbalance of humors, or when we navigated the turbulent waters of civil rights legislation in the face of deeply ingrained prejudices. It was intellectual humility that fueled our progress along these treacherous paths.

An essential aspect of intellectual humility is the willingness to change our beliefs when presented with rigorous evidence that contradicts our precon-ceived notions. It is not merely that we accept our fallibility; ultimately, this understanding must guide us towards a genuine commitment to adapt and evolve.

Our world today abounds with myriad sources of knowledge, allowing us to examine perspectives that were once out of our reach. However, this wealth of information also necessitates increased vigilance, as our cognitive biases can beckon us down the path of least resistance, allowing us to cherry-pick only that which confirms our pre-existing beliefs. To choose otherwise requires effort, courage, and an insatiable curiosity for what lies beyond our mental horizons. It mandates that we swap the comforting garb of certainty for the disquieting cloak of perpetual questioning.

Consider the historical episodes of those who challenged the status quo and the seemingly "indisputable" truths of their time. Galileo Galilei, the brilliant Italian polymath, had the audacity - some might say the temerity - to defend the heliocentric model of the universe when everyone around him firmly believed in the Earth's centrality. Despite facing persecution, an unwavering Galileo dared to question, examine, and eventually amend the human understanding of the cosmos. It is this caliber of intellectual curiosity, courage, and adaptability that we need to emulate.

The willingness to change one's beliefs when confronted with new evidence offers a cascade of benefits. On an individual level, it is this intellectual pliability that keeps us from stagnating, sparking perpetual growth and refinement of understanding. It alleviates the pressure to always be "right," freeing us to undertake a grander exploration of the ever-evolving tapestry of knowledge.

Moreover, our capacity to confront and assimilate evidence leads to the redressing of incorrect beliefs and enables us to craft solutions better suited to the challenges facing our society. Questions of public health, climate change, and social disparities demand that we remain vigilant in our quest for the truth and steadfast in our commitment to adapt and change when confronted with reliable evidence. By merging intellectual humility with a willingness to act upon the knowledge we gain, we can steer the world towards a brighter future fueled by evidence, empathy, and wisdom.

In tandem with the willingness to change our beliefs in light of new evidence, intellectual humility mandates that we recognize and accept the finite nature of our knowledge and expertise. We must embrace the epistemological truth that no matter how well-versed we are in a particular domain, our understanding of the vast expanse of human knowledge will always remain partial.

This realization forces us to confront the inherent limitations of our intellectual capacities and vantage points, making us aware that others may hold insights that can complete, complement or even challenge our own understanding. It means nurturing a collaborative spirit and drawing on the expertise of others as we strive to refine our worldview and forge a collective truth.

We inhabit a world of increasing interdependence and interconnectedness, with the challenges we face becoming more complex and the significance of isolated expertise diminishing. In this intricate landscape, we must learn to build upon one another's understandings, inventing solutions that are pooled from multiple disciplines and perspectives.

The recognition of the limits of individual knowledge and expertise is both humbling and empowering. It liberates us from the burden of having to know it all, permitting us to hone our unique talents while gaining the ability to collaborate effectively with others. Moreover, it fosters empathy and diminishes ego, as we learn to appreciate and value the insights of our fellow global citizens.

3

Cherry-picking the evidence

As we delve deeper into the nuanced landscape where intellectual humility and human error converge, we reacquaint ourselves with the complex cognitive phenomenon known as confirmation bias. This psychological inclination lures us into pursuing information that resonates with our pre-existing beliefs, while simultaneously nudging us to discard or overlook evidence that challenges our perceived certainties. This deceptively potent bias imperceptibly distorts our grasp on reality, tempting us to handpick evidence that caters to our convictions, frequently undermining the precision and dependability of our understanding of the world.

Imagine a mechanic examining a malfunctioning engine. If she's convinced that the issue lies with the transmission, she might spend hours investigating that component, all the while overlooking the real culprit: a faulty spark plug. Even when presented with data suggestive of the true defect, her initial conviction may render her blind to the contradictory evidence before her.

This tendency to reinforce our existing beliefs becomes particularly problematic when our convictions are rooted in deep-seated emotions or identity. It compels us to actively seek out sources that validate our opinions and steer away from those that challenge them, effectively constructing an echo chamber of affirmation, where our ideas are continually reinforced and never critically examined.

In the realm of politics, for example, confirmation bias can drive people of differing ideologies further apart, as they gravitate towards news sources, articles, and commentaries that confirm their own partisan views, leaving little room for engaging with opposing perspectives. This behavioral pattern spurs polarization and fosters animosity, effectively stymieing meaningful discussion and understanding between disparate groups.

Not only does confirmation bias compel us to cling to our beliefs, but it engenders a stubborn resistance to change, even when new information or a fresh perspective could potentially broaden our understanding of a given subject. Our attachment to pre-existing opinions can become a cognitive straitjacket, constricting our receptivity and adaptability to novel ideas.

Consider the classic Aesop's fable of the Crow and the Pitcher. When a thirsty crow stumbles upon a pitcher containing a small amount of water, it endures the arduous task of gathering and dropping pebbles into the vessel, one by one, to raise the water level high enough to drink. By embracing innovation and adaptively responding to a challenge, the crow ultimately triumphs.

However, when we become inflexible in our beliefs, clinging stubbornly to our predispositions, we risk overlooking potentially viable solutions to the problems we face. Confirmation bias fosters a reluctance to reconsider our stances, preventing us from seeking out the pebbles that may raise the water of our understanding.

Picture the scene: It's the early 1980s in America, and a moral panic is taking root, fueled by sensationalist media, anxieties about societal change, and the active imaginations of concerned citizens. It's a time when the United States, much like the rest of the world, is undergoing a period of significant transformation. The Cold War looms in the background, technology is advancing at breakneck speed, and youth culture is pushing the boundaries of longstanding norms. Enter the Satanic Panic, a remarkable and shocking frenzy that ultimately serves as a case study in confirmation bias and how it can lead even the brightest minds down the path of reason-strayed folly.

At the heart of the Satanic Panic lay the absurd notion that a vast, secretive network of Satan-worshiping individuals roamed the nation, kidnapping and sacrificing innocent children, committing crimes, and engaging in disturbing rituals. Thanks to a mix of religious zealotry, cultural anxieties, and overactive imaginations, these allegations swept through the public consciousness like wildfire.

It all began with a few initial claims, but soon, people started seeing evidence of satanic activity everywhere. This was confirmation bias at its most potent: once individuals had embraced the belief that Satanists were operating in their communities, they sought out and seized upon any piece of information that might substantiate this fear. Bizarre doodles found in a child's notebook? It must be a satanic symbol. A teenager experimenting with heavy metal music and alternative fashion? Clearly, they were on the brink of recruitment by a satanic cult. With each new "finding," the fear factor escalated.

At the same time, various "experts" emerged, asserting their ability to identify signs of satanic activity and grooming. Shoddy science, question-able methods, and dubious qualifications did not deter law enforcement, therapists, and school administrators from consulting with these so-called specialists. Additionally, many of these authorities held education seminars, perpetuating their own particular biases while claiming to offer unbiased guidance.

A critical turning point in the Satanic Panic saga came in 1983 with The McMartin Preschool trial, which stands out as one of the longest and most expensive criminal trials in American history. Accused of horrifying acts against the children in their care, the case caused widespread panic, despite glaring weaknesses in the collected evidence.

The first allegations were brought forth by Judy Johnson, who claimed that her son had been sexually abused by Ray Buckey, a teacher at the McMartin Preschool in Manhattan Beach, California. Johnson's claims spiraled into a much larger investigation, with over 360 children accusing Buckey and six other school staff members of participating in bizarre and gruesome rituals that bore the imagined hallmarks of a satanic cult.

Investigators turned to a questionable method called "anatomically correct doll interviews," which were intended to help children disclose vital information about their alleged abusers. However, these doll-based interviews created an environment ripe for suggestion and led children to describe outlandish events with little grounding in reality, leading to more false accusations and misinterpretations, creating a vicious cycle of unfounded fears and faulty evidence. Many of the children's allegations were contradictory, which should have raised red flags for law enforcement and prosecution.

In their rush to believe these stories (and at the behest of sensationalist media coverage), key participants in the case overlooked the lack of physical evidence connecting defendants to these alleged crimes. This judicial blindness was compounded by increasingly desperate measures to substantiate the accusations, with authorities even turning to untrained and unqualified "experts" in the occult to validate unfounded claims.

After a seven-year long legal battle, all charges were dismissed due to insufficient evidence, and the accused teachers' lives were left in shambles. This outcome was undoubtedly a victory for the accused, but the damage done to their reputations and the countless judicial resources expended in the pursuit of an imagined conspiracy could never be undone. The McMartin case is a stark reminder of the destructive power of fear and hysteria, as well as the importance of due process and reliance on credible evidence.

Many people, from parents to law enforcement officials, succumbed to the hysteria and failed to critically analyze the evidence before them. Confirmation bias perpetuated fear and panic, wreaking havoc on those falsely accused in the process.

Fast forward to the present day, and we find ourselves grappling with another, arguably more insidious, consequence of widespread unchecked confirmation bias: political polarization and the spread of misinformation, particularly via social media platforms. This growing divide has fractured communities, magnified extremes, and made it increasingly difficult to hold meaningful conversations across ideological lines. This time around, our sources of news and information—and the ease with which we can access content that confirms our biases—lie at the center of this complex modern phenomenon.

The rise of the internet and social media has fundamentally altered the way we consume news and information. In many ways, this shift has led to greater democratization and broader access to a variety of perspectives. However, it has also made it easier for users to fall into the trap of confirmation bias, as algorithms—which increasingly dictate what content we encounter and engage with—reward us for seeking out and engaging with ideas that resonate with our pre-existing beliefs.

Our Facebook feeds, Twitter timelines, and curated news apps become digital echo chambers that feed our confirmation bias, offering up an endless stream of articles, think-pieces, and shared experiences that align with our views of the world. We become trapped in these feedback loops, reading and sharing stories that align with our perspectives while dismissing articles that challenge our ideological stances. Over time, this cycle hardens our positions, erodes our empathy, and widens the chasm between differing viewpoints.

Furthermore, this dynamic has amplified the spread of misinformation, conspiracy theories, and so-called "fake news." Social media platforms, thanks to their vast reach and targeted advertising, offer a powerful means of disseminating falsehoods that appeal to and validate our biases. Consider the phenomenon of "deep fakes," where manipulated videos are deliberately created to generate outrage or confusion, often clouding the distinction between what is real and what is not. Unverified sources and unsubstantiated claims often spread rapidly and as a result, distort our collective understanding of events and issues.

For many, the allure of confirmation bias is not just the comfort that comes with having one's beliefs confirmed, but also the appeal of joining an ideologically-aligned community. This emotion is rooted in our evolutionary tendencies; we're social animals, and we seek out like-minded individuals to reinforce and validate our worldviews. This natural inclination can be both a blessing and a curse, especially in an era of hyper-polarization.

One platform that has risen in popularity for fostering these insular communities is the largely unmoderated instant messaging app, Telegram. Originally created as a secure communication tool with a focus on privacy, the platform has gained a reputation for enabling closed groups and channels dedicated to the spread of misinformation and disinformation.

The hidden nature of these groups allows bad information to grow unchallenged, free from the scrutiny of dissenting voices or fact-checking mechanisms. Members of these groups are free to reinforce each other's distorted worldviews, amplifying the impact of confirmation bias and fostering an environment where critical thinking takes a back seat to validating one's existing beliefs.

A striking example of this phenomenon occurred during the 2020 U.S. presidential election, when Telegram channels bolstered and amplified dangerous misinformation surrounding election fraud claims. An investigation into one such group exposed a toxic ecosystem wherein conspiracy theories, debunked claims, and outright falsehoods were shared and propagated amongst the members, completely insulated from outside fact-checkers or dissenting viewpoints. This group, which had thousands of members, became a breeding ground for disinformation, perpetuating a false narrative and fueling mistrust in the democratic process.

The closed nature of these groups also makes it difficult to ascertain the source of the misinformation—whether it is genuine misunderstanding, deliberate manipulation, or foreign interference. Regardless of the origin, the result is the same: a tide of misinformation that continues to swell and erode trust in institutions and experts, while widening social and political divides.

The impact of confirmation bias extends even to the hallowed halls of scientific research, where you might expect researchers' dedication to objectivity and the scientific method to prevent such distortions from taking root. Unfortunately, even in this domain, confirmation bias and its cousin, publication bias, can suffuse the process of discovery and erect barriers on the road to new knowledge. By shining a light on how these biases manifest in the realm of academia, we can better understand where we need to bolster the scientific process and rediscover the ideals of curiosity-driven inquiry.

Scientists aren't immune to the grip of confirmation bias when it comes to designing experiments, interpreting data, and putting their findings forth to the rest of the scientific community. An implicit (or sometimes explicit) pressure to deliver positive results nudges researchers towards methods that might favor the confirmation of their hypotheses. This motivation can result in a type of cognitive shortcut known as "p-hacking," where a researcher manipulates data or tinkers with statistical techniques until they find a statistically significant result that supports their theory. In such cases, the results may be anything but objective or generalizable, but they still end up published and cited, fueling future lines of investigation built on shaky foundations.

This problem is exacerbated by the existence of publication bias, a distortion in which scientific journals—driven by their quest for impact and reader-ship—opt for publishing predominantly significant and positive findings. Studies that confirm hypotheses or demonstrate strong effects tend to have a higher likelihood of being accepted for publication, while null or inconclusive results may languish unread in file drawers or fail to make it even that far. This bias paints a distorted portrait of the prevailing research landscape, with only the most exciting and hypothesis-confirming results rising to the top, while underpowered or contradictory studies remain under the radar.

One disquieting illustration of the implications of publication bias can be found in the widespread use of antidepressants. For decades, research on depression and its treatments has been dogged by publication bias, with studies demonstrating the efficacy of pharmaceutical interventions being far more likely to see the light of day than those that found little to no benefit in the efficacy of these drugs. As a result, the effectiveness of these medications was considerably overstated, and many patients were prescribed potentially unnecessary and costly treatment regimens, based on a skewed understanding of the research.

Scientists and the institutions that support them are not blind to this world of p-hacking and publication bias, and efforts are now being made to mitigate their influence. Researchers have adopted transparent methods, like pre-registering their hypotheses before gathering data and using open science initiatives that emphasize publishing all results—positive, negative, or inconclusive—and sharing data and methodological details more openly. By adopting these forward-thinking approaches, the scientific community can break free of the vicious cycle of confirmation bias and publication bias, and instead set their sights on the reliable advancement of human knowledge.

Effectively addressing these biases at the heart of science — where every new discovery has profound implications for society — shines as an example that illustrates just how important it is to tackle the issue of confirmation bias wherever it may arise. When we loosen the grip of confirmation bias on our collective intellect, we not only protect ourselves from misinformation and polarization but also, crucially, pave the way for the unearthing of genuine insights that can shape our world for the better.

4

Why being too sure can go wrong

In a world fraught with uncertainty and ambiguity, confidence can be a valuable and even necessary asset. The authoritative leader who inspires with their unshakable belief in a cause, the entrepreneur who launches a risky venture with unwavering conviction—these stories captivate our imaginations and seduce us into a romance with unbridled self-assuredness. However, there is a shadowy side to confidence that, if left unchecked, may result in the very undoing of our cherished ambitions. This shadow takes the form of the overconfidence effect, a cognitive bias that leads us to overestimate our abilities and the accuracy of our beliefs, even in the face of weighty evidence to the contrary.

At its core, the overconfidence effect stems from a natural proclivity to harbor an inflated sense of our own knowledge, skills, and expertise. This psychological phenomenon manifests in three key ways: overestimation, where we think we are better at a task than we actually are; overplacement, where we believe we are superior to others in a particular domain; and overprecision, where we are overly certain about the accuracy of our beliefs and predictions. Far from being limited to the realm of narcissists or egomaniacs, the overconfidence effect pervades the everyday cognition of even the most humble among us.

Why does this pervasive bias hold such sway over our minds? In part, it can be traced back to our brain's aversion to the ambiguity and anxiety that comes with acknowledging our own limitations and the murkiness of our judgments. As sentient beings, we are wired to seek patterns, create order from chaos, and forge connections that will help us navigate the world. A sustained sense of confidence can help ward off the creeping dread that might otherwise paralyze us in the face of uncertainty. Yet the mind's eagerness to weave a comforting narrative from the threads of our experiences, beliefs, and desires can blind us to the true extent of our ignorance.

Overconfidence is also fueled by our proclivity to selectively recall the instances where our judgments have proven correct, creating a distorted mental highlight reel that reinforces our elevated self-perception. When we update our beliefs, the process may be further skewed by our tendency to interpret new evidence as confirmation of our preexisting notions, a dynamic we have already explored in the context of confirmation bias.

Understanding the overconfidence effect requires examining how our personalities and expertise contribute to our frequent flirtations with this beguiling cognitive pitfall. It would be tempting to ascribe overconfidence to particular character traits or fields of expertise, perhaps allowing us to isolate and quarantine the phenomenon in a specific subset of the population. Yet the truth is far more complex and far-reaching than such convenient explanations might suggest.

Personality, it turns out, plays a nuanced role in fostering overconfidence. People with dominant and assertive dispositions – those who exude natural leadership qualities – might indeed be more prone to overestimating their competence in social and professional settings. However, humility, often considered the antithesis of overconfidence, is not an automatic safeguard against bias. Even those who describe themselves as modest, self-effacing, or aware of their own limitations can still unwittingly succumb to overconfidence in specific domains or under particular circumstances.

When it comes to expertise and experience, the role they play in shaping overconfidence is both intriguing and cautionary. One might assume that the more skilled or knowledgeable individuals would be immune to this particular brand of cognitive distortion. However, greater expertise may sometimes engender its own unique flavor of overconfidence. Experts, having garnered considerable recognition and a sense of self-assuredness in their milieu, might paradoxically be more susceptible to the allure of overprecision or overplacement. This vulnerability arises from an entrenched credibility in the domain, a sense of earned authority, and the lure of projecting unwavering certainty.

Novices, on the other hand, are not without their own peculiar susceptibility to overconfidence. Unaware of the full extent of their inexperience, these individuals may fall victim to the so-called "Beginner's Luck" syndrome, where early successes or facile encounters can induce an inflated sense of mastery that does not correspond to their actual abilities. Instances where luck and circumstance may have played a role in success become obscured by the brain's propensity for self-congratulatory narratives, breeding overestimation.

This intricate interplay between personality and expertise nuances the broad strokes with which we might be tempted to paint the overconfidence effect. Both the reticent introvert and the commanding extrovert, the seasoned expert and the enthusiastic neophyte – all may, in their own unique ways, be courted by the seductive whispers of overconfidence as they grapple with the uncertainty and ambiguity of the human condition.

The tragedy of the Titanic, that ill-fated maiden voyage, offers a palpable illustration of the pernicious influence of overconfidence. The luxurious ocean liner was the largest and most technologically advanced vessel of its time, boasting state-of-the-art safety features and amenities. It was an unprecedented marvel, the embodiment of human ingenuity, ambition, and progress. Yet in its tragic wake, the Titanic remains forever a symbol of hubris and the fragile boundary between self-assurance and self-destruction.

The architects, engineers, and crew responsible for the conception, construction, and navigation of the Titanic were certainly not without expertise or experience. In fact, they were among the foremost experts in their respective fields, and for good reason. It was precisely this extraordinary collective competence that sustained the prevailing belief – the vision of an unsinkable ship, impervious to both human error and the whims of the capricious North Atlantic.

This confidence was not entirely baseless, born from a deep understanding of naval architecture and maritime navigation. Yet as the Titanic slipped beneath the icy waves in the early hours of April 15, 1912, the unthinkable truth emerged – a veritable testament to the pitfalls of unwavering overconfidence.

The consequences of this excessive faith in the capabilities of the Titanic are myriad and well-documented. Rampant speculation abounds regarding the voyage's fateful final hours, touching on myriad points of failure – from the insufficient stock of lifeboats and the absence of binoculars for lookouts to the ignored iceberg warnings and the excessive speed at which the ship traversed the perilous waters.

Yet each of these factors, while critical, belies a more insidious and elusive truth. These pivotal missteps were not willful acts of negligence or conscious slights, but the natural byproducts of a broader societal overconfidence in the capabilities of the ship. The Titanic was to be the ultimate triumph of reason over adversity, a shining emblem of mankind's undeniable mastery over the elemental forces of nature.

The true power of the Titanic story lies not in the intricate complexity of its causes or the grim details of its aftermath, but in its ability to illuminate the remarkable capacity of individuals – even those at the very pinnacle of their respective fields – to lapse into illusions of invincibility. This iconic tale not only exposes the omnipresent risks surrounding the overconfidence effect, but also serves as a timeless exhortation to remain vigilant against the encroaching tendrils of unchecked self-assurance, lest we too find ourselves falling victim to the folly of our own making.

The catastrophic global financial crisis of 2008, an economic earthquake that shook the very foundations of the world's most robust economies, provides another stark example of overconfidence run amok. At its core, this staggering financial collapse can be traced back to a virulent strain of overconfidence – a shared belief that the storied architects of modern finance had tamed the unruly forces of the market with their newfound, almost mystical understanding of complex mathematical models and risk management strategies.

In the years leading up to the crisis, Wall Street was abuzz with excitement over the ingenious innovation of securitization – the process of pooling and repackaging loans into bundles that could then be sold as securities to investors. Among these financial instruments, mortgage-backed securities garnered unprecedented attention, turning American homeowners' mortgage debt into a lucrative gold mine for both banks and institutional investors.

The true allure of these securities, however, lay not in their intrinsic value but in their presumed capacity to effortlessly disperse risk. Through sophisticated financial engineering, salient market players peddled the perception that these novel instruments had successfully neutralized and domesticated the unruly forces of financial uncertainty. The market, once a bewildering and unpredictable beast, had been tamed into submission. Or so they believed.

Imbued with this intoxicating confidence, bankers, regulators, and investors alike were blind to the gathering storm clouds on the horizon. The subprime mortgage market, a highly vulnerable segment composed of borrowers with poor credit history, was rapidly inflating into an unsustainable bubble. Profits soared and buoyed by their own perceived invincibility, the market participants continued to place risky bets, certain that their power over the financial ecosystem could withstand any conceivable turmoil.

And then, in the fateful year of 2008, the bubble burst. The value of mortgage-backed securities collapsed, triggering catastrophic, chain-reaction failures across the global financial sector. As the dust settled, the sobering reality became clear – the illusion of control, born from an all-consuming overconfidence in the capabilities and expertise of the financial elite, had left the entire global economy precariously imperiled.

The chilling legacy of the 2008 financial crisis galvanizes the lessons gleaned from the Titanic disaster, reminding us yet again of the perils of an unchecked overconfidence effect. In the face of unprecedented advancements and innovations, we must not succumb to the siren song of infallibility, but rather, strive to remain profoundly self-aware and steadfastly vigilant against the invisible ravages of our own intellectual hubris.

5

The hold of first impressions

Amidst the ever-shifting currents of human thought and reason, a powerful yet oft-overlooked influence quietly shapes our perceptions and decision-making processes: the anchoring bias. Like an unseen magnet, this cognitive pitfall subtly pulls and distorts our thinking, often with profound consequences for our lives and the wider world. To fully comprehend the importance of intellectual humility, we must delve deeper into this fascinating psychological phenomenon and discern how it wields its unseen grip upon our psyches.

Anchoring bias, at its essence, results from our innate cognitive tendency to latch onto the first piece of information we encounter – be it a fact, figure, or impression – and utilize it as a reference point from which we subsequently base our judgments. This initial "anchor" becomes so ingrained in our minds that it sways our future assessments, even when presented with new and potentially more relevant data. The potency of this cognitive trap lies in its insidious subtlety, for we often remain wholly unaware of the sway it holds.

The psychological underpinnings of anchoring bias can be traced to the workings of the mind's two systems of cognitive processing: System 1 and System 2. System 1, characterized by its rapid, automatic, and effortless mode of operation, forms our intuitive and heuristic judgments. In contrast, System 2 engages with information deliberately and analytically, consuming considerable cognitive resources. Anchoring bias emerges when the swift and efficient System 1 operates in tandem with the more rational System 2, creating an unconscious tug-of-war between intuition and logic that skews our decision-making process.

One might wonder how such an imperceptible force could exert such vast consequences upon our lives. However, as we dive into the labyrinthine workings of anchoring bias, we witness its effects rippling across myriad domains, from our financial decisions and political beliefs to our personal relationships and career trajectories. Our propensity to cleave to that initial anchor point in our minds runs deep, for it is deeply entwined with our psychological makeup.

To understand the pervasive influence of anchoring on our perceptions, we must first examine how it operates within the vast and complex mosaic of everyday life. Anchoring takes root when we navigate through the torrent of information that bombards our senses, embedding itself within the choices we make and the beliefs we hold dear. Like an invisible puppet-master, it deftly maneuvers the strings of our thoughts and judgments, often undetected in the recesses of our cognition.

In the realm of economics and consumer behavior, the effects of anchoring are starkly apparent. Consider, for instance, the price tags that sway a shopper's decision-making. Retailers often exploit the anchoring bias by setting high initial prices for their products, creating a reference point in the mind of the consumer that magnifies the perceived value of subsequent discounts. With little more than a bolded number on a tag or a strategic mention of the original price, consumers are lured into the illusion of a sale, when in reality, the discount may not be as substantial as it first appears. Within the financial markets, anchoring bias also rears its head as investors cling to an unrealistically high past price, unwilling to reconcile their expectations with shifting market trends, leading to potentially costly decisions.

Anchoring exerts its influence well beyond the marketplace; it permeates our personal and professional relationships as well. First impressions often act as powerful anchors, coloring our subsequent interactions and evaluations of others. In a job interview, for example, the initial presence of a well-polished resume or an air of confidence and charm may create an anchor that sees the candidate in a favorable light, even if later revelations expose weaknesses in their experience or character. Likewise, in matters of the heart, anchoring can dictate the course of our romantic relationships – as a first date filled with chemistry and connection may overshadow or excuse subsequent discord that arises between the partners.

The tendrils of anchoring reach into the sobering sphere of politics as well. Voters may fixate upon a particular candidate's stance on a single issue, allowing that anchor to influence their perception of that candidate's overall qualifications and suitability to lead. This cognitive blind spot can lead to situations where crucial information on other policies and character traits becomes obscured, critically marring the voter's ability to make informed decisions.

Delving deeper into the domain of high-stakes negotiations and consequential business transactions, the insidious influence of anchoring bias conceals itself in the subtle details of the exchange. Any negotiation unfolds as a dynamic interplay between the parties involved, each side hoping to achieve the best possible outcome. Unknown to many, the outcome is often swayed by the stealthy hand of anchoring, which dictates the terms and parameters of the negotiation before a single word is uttered.

Imagine yourself in the midst of a negotiation for the purchase of a company. As the buyer, you hold certain expectations about the company's value, and as any skilled negotiator would, you set an opening bid well below that estimate, hoping to achieve a favorable outcome. However, unbeknownst to you, that initial figure has already begun to manipulate the entire course of the negotiation. It whispers in the ears of the sellers, leading them through a mental dance where the anchor takes center stage. They now perceive your proposal as the reference point, adjusting their expectations accordingly.

This dance of anchoring bias knows no bounds. In the labyrinth of salary negotiations, an employer might propose a starting wage far below the market rate, enticing the prospective employee to adjust their expectations, while unknowingly forfeiting thousands of dollars of potential income. In real estate transactions too, the anchoring effect manifests as listing prices communicate an implicit value of the property, nudging potential homebuyers to adjust their perception and offers to align with that reference point.

It is not that the parties involved in these negotiations are intentionally planting anchors, but rather that the seeds of anchoring are sown automatically, concealing themselves in the very fabric of the conversation. Indeed, even the most well-intentioned negotiator may fall prey to the anchoring bias, even if unaware of its presence.

In seeking to retain clarity amidst the haze of anchoring biases that cloud our judgment in business transactions, a disciplined mind must question not only the origins of the anchors but also the validity of the reference points they create. By arming ourselves with more extensive information and engaging in critical reflection, we can better navigate the intricate landscape of negotiations without the undue influence clouding our vision.

In the solemn domain of the courtroom, where lives hang in the balance and the weight of justice is palpable, one might presume that the cerebral and considered minds of judges and juries would remain immune to the reach of the anchoring bias. Alas, even within these hallowed halls, where reason and truth are held in the highest esteem, the influence of anchoring cannot be so easily banished, subtly shaping the deliberations and verdicts of those entrusted with some of our society's most critical decisions.

Let us turn our attention to the process of sentencing in criminal trials. At face value, the determination of punitive measures might appear to be a matter of calculated logic and dispassionate assessment, driven by stringent guidelines and informed by the merits of each case. Yet, as we peel back the layers of judicial procedure, we unveil the hidden threads of anchoring that weave their way into the fabric of justice, tainting verdicts and swaying outcomes.

For instance, consider the crucial role that sentencing recommendations play in influencing the final decisions of judges. In providing a suggestion of a fitting punishment for a convicted criminal, the prosecution unwittingly plants the seed of anchoring in the soil of the judge's mind. From that moment forward, the judge's thoughts and deliberations inevitably become tethered to that initial anchor, affecting their decisions as they strive to approximate an appropriate sentence.

Similarly, even where a sentencing range is prescribed by regulation or statute, the judge remains vulnerable to the anchoring effect. For example, the subtle cues provided by the upper or lower boundaries of the range—or the midpoint, for that matter—may act as potent reference points, guiding the judge's decision towards those inherently arbitrary values.

The pernicious nature of anchoring impacts not only the judgments of legal professionals but also those of laypersons serving as jurors. Indeed, numerical values whispered in the testimonies of witnesses and experts alike can inadvertently lay the groundwork for anchors, shaping jurors' perceptions of what is fair, just, or reasonable. Burdened with the responsibility of deciding both guilt and compensatory awards, jurors are susceptible to these unseen whispers that speak to their innermost thoughts and judgements.

This realization invites introspection, urging those who ply the halls of justice to confront the silent puppeteer of anchoring which dances behind the austere façade of the courtroom. Acknowledging the presence of this surreptitious bias, judges, jurors, and lawyers alike must strive to mitigate its impact, cultivating an intellectual humility that challenges the status quo and elevates the integrity of our justice system. In doing so, they champion a pursuit of truth untethered from the insidious sway of the anchoring bias.

6

The influence of memory on our judgment

Embarking on the realm of the availability heuristic, we find a psychological principle with deceptively subtle yet profound implications on our decision-making processes. While the term itself might be less familiar, we often unwittingly subscribe to its influence in the interstice of our day-to-day lives. To truly grasp the significance of the availability heuristic, we must first venture into its essence and establish a comprehensive understanding of its inner workings.

The availability heuristic, a term coined by psychologists Amos Tversky and Daniel Kahneman, refers to the cognitive shortcut our minds take when estimating the probability or frequency of an event by relying on information that is readily accessible to us, whether it be a recent memory or the most vivid of experiences. This mental agility facilitates decision-making in situations of uncertainty, allowing us to navigate through the myriad possibilities with ease and intuition.

However, this heuristic comes with its share of caveats and imperfections, for the information summoned by our minds does not always align with the objective reality. In essence, our propensity to seize upon easily retrievable data may inadvertently cloud the accuracy of our estimations, as these accessible fragments may not necessarily represent the broader landscape of facts and figures.

It is helpful to envision the availability heuristic as a form of cognitive triage, a mental mechanism that allows us to quickly sift through the complex matrix of our memories and experiences to find those that appear most relevant and significant at a given moment. Yet, like any triage, there exists an inherent possibility of prioritizing the wrong criteria or overlooking subtler pieces of vital information. This is particularly true when we are swayed by the potency of emotions or the razzle-dazzle of sensationalism often found in news headlines and anecdotes shared amongst friends.

To further unravel the intricacies of the availability heuristic, we turn to the interplay between memory, attention, and the unconscious shaping of our decisions. Like a beguiling waltz, these aspects of the mind dance together in complex rhythms, complementing and influencing one another as we attempt to decipher the world around us.

Our memories form an intricate tapestry of experiences, emotions, and facts, woven together by the threads of time. And yet, not every square inch of our memory tapestry is readily accessible to us when needed. We are often guided by our attention to specific segments carved out by the immediacy of our experiences, the intensity of our emotions, and the magnetism of vivid recollections. Ephemeral moments can be more memorable than commonplace occurrences—an exotic yet terrifying adventure may persist in our thoughts more readily than the countless days of familiar routines.

Attention, in essence, is a spotlight that directs our cognitive resources towards particular phenomena, tailored by the intricate interconnections of our memories. The web of associations that envelop our thoughts gravitates our focus towards those fleeting moments, emotional experiences, and sensational images that imprint themselves in our minds. These are the pieces of information that are often the easiest to conjure up, seducing us into the realm of the availability heuristic.

Ironically, it is in these moments of intense focus that the potential cracks in the seemingly unbreakable grip of the availability heuristic are illuminated. These moments that take precedence in our mental survey might inadvertently create a distortion in how we perceive reality—an availability bias if you will. This bias inclines us to overestimate the prevalence and importance of the events and situations that draw our attention, while systematically underestimating those that tread in the quiet shadows of our memory banks.

A curious intersection between the availability heuristic, memory, and attention emerges when we delve into the realm of media coverage and the shaping of perceptions around crime and safety. As we become immersed in a sea of headlines clamoring for our attention, the theatrical dance of memory and attention centers our thoughts on the stories that heighten our emotions and ignite a primal fear deep within our subconscious.

Despite statistics showing that crime rates have been steadily decreasing for decades in many countries, people's perception of their safety is anything but accurate. Media outlets, vying for ratings and clicks from eager consumers, latch onto the most frightening and visceral stories of crime and violence, broadcasting them directly into our homes and digital devices. Through this deluge of terrifying and sensational news, our mind's attentional spotlight gravitates unwittingly toward these more vivid, fear-inducing tales—a fertile breeding ground for the availability heuristic to flourish.

The repetitive presentation of such media content, coupled with our brains' innate predisposition to focus on emotionally stimulating material, leaves a lasting impression on our memory tapestry. Entranced by the vivid scenes of crime and unrest, we begin to form a mental shortcut, associating the frequency of these stories with the general state of safety in society. What appears prevalent on our screens grows distorted roots in our minds, creating a warped perception that crime is more rampant than it truly is.

Decision-making, in turn, cannot help but be affected by these distorted perceptions. Individuals might justify increased surveillance and stringent law enforcement or indulge in unnecessary security measures—installing expensive alarms, purchasing guns, or even relocating to "safer" areas. Society, responding to this collective anxiety, echoes these personal decisions with policy changes, resource allocation, and amplified racial and socioeconomic tensions.

The ripple effects of these individual and societal responses to perceived threats can create a feedback loop of fear, altering the very fabric of society. Historical events exemplify the massive implications of this phenomenon in action. The tragic events of September 11th, 2001 forever changed the American landscape, planting the seeds of fear in the hearts and minds of people around the world. The harrowing images of the Twin Towers collapsing and the loss of nearly 3,000 lives remain scorched into the collective memory—an indisputable testament to the potency of the availability heuristic.

In the days and weeks that followed the terrorist attacks, the media fed the public's unquenchable thirst for coverage of these horrific events. Saturated with replays of the falling towers, reports of airport security breaches, and glowing profiles of the terrorists, society began to view air travel with trepidation—convinced that stepping onto an airplane was an invitation to the grim reaper.

As our minds fixated on the vivid specter of another 9/11, unrecognized dangers began to multiply in the shadows. A study by German economist Gerd Gigerenzer, director of the Max Planck Institute for Human Development, illuminated one such unseen peril. Gigerenzer reported that, in the year following the terrorist attacks, an estimated 1,595 additional American lives were lost on the roads as fearful travelers swapped airplanes for automobiles.

The irony is both tragic and profound: By avoiding the perceived danger of flying, people unwittingly chose a mode of transport that, statistically speaking, had higher accident rates. This unsettling case exemplifies how the grim dance between memory, attention, and the availability heuristic can lead us to faulty conclusions and questionable decision-making.

What this phenomenon reveals is that amidst the torrent of emotionally charged media coverage, our attention was overwhelmed by the daunting prospect of another terrorist attack. The sheer intensity of the events effectively obscured the statistical reality—that the odds of being a victim of a terrorist attack, even in the wake of 9/11, were infinitesimally small compared to the risks of driving a car.

These unanswered questions loom large: How many lives could have been saved if our perceptions had properly aligned with reality? How might we cultivate a more nuanced understanding of risk that acknowledges the biases that lurk within our own minds?

7

The danger of consensus without examination

In the heart of this exploration into the human psyche lies an enigmatic force, one that arises from the very essence of our social nature. It is a subtle distortion of collective wisdom—a metamorphosis of shared deliberation into a dangerous web of faulty decision-making. This force, known as groupthink, is a peculiar infirmity that eclipses even the sharpest minds and has led to staggering misjudgments across history.

To unravel the intricate workings of groupthink, we must first establish a clear definition. Coined by social psychologist Irving Janis in 1972, the term "groupthink" refers to a mode of thinking characterized by poor decision-making and tunnel vision within a group, driven by an overwhelming desire for harmony, conformity, and consensus.

At its core, groupthink originates from the natural, undeniable human yearning for acceptance and validation, deeply ingrained within our social instincts. Hence, it stems from a profound fear of being ostracized or ridiculed by the very factions to which we pledge allegiance. In this realm of self-preservation, dissent is disregarded as disloyalty, stifling the precious oxygen of independent thought and, in turn, suffocating the group's ability to scrutinize decisions critically.

The psychological machinery that drives groupthink involves cognitive biases, social dynamics, and organizational factors. Confirmation bias plays a pivotal role in perpetuating groupthink. Groups caught in this snare primarily seek out and prioritize information that aligns with their prevailing views while dismissing contradictory evidence. This perilous tendency allows groupthink to flourish, as members construct a shared narrative comprising handpicked "facts," devoid of any discordant tones.

The mechanics of groupthink are further fueled by social identity theory and the basic human need to belong to a group that shares similar beliefs and values. When the shared identity and cohesion of a group face potential fragmentation due to disagreement, members tend to abandon their critical faculties and yield to the seductive lure of unanimity. Thus, the drive for belonging supersedes the pursuit of rationality, rendering the group susceptible to distorted judgment.

Now that we have delved into the psychological roots of groupthink, let us shift our focus to the external circumstances and dynamics that invite its unwelcome presence. Although all groups are susceptible to falling into the trap of groupthink, certain conditions undoubtedly amplify its influence.

One such factor is a strong, persuasive leader who wields considerable control over the group's decision-making process. Under such leadership, the craving for cohesion and the dread of dissent escalate, as members strive to please the revered figure at the helm. Though initially, this submission may appear benign, it turns insidious when all contrary perspectives are flattened, leaving behind an echo chamber devoid of critical evaluation.

Groupthink can also be engendered by an atmosphere of isolation. When a group is separated—whether physically or figuratively—from external influences or alternative viewpoints, it becomes confined within the boundaries of its own assumptions and ideologies. This seclusion nurtures a fertile ground for groupthink's emergence, as the collective consciousness narrows and converges on a single-minded path.

Another contributing factor is the presence of high pressure and stress within the group. When confronted with urgent deadlines, crisis situations, or momentous decisions, the instinct to veer towards conformity tends to heighten, suppressing the exploration of diverse alternatives. Amidst the weight of expectations and impending consequences, the desire to avoid disagreements and delays in decision-making becomes paramount, thus paving the way for groupthink's encroachment.

Lastly, homogeneous group composition, in terms of background, experience, and perspective, actively breeds the susceptibility to groupthink. Immersed in a pool of like-minded individuals, members become prone to mutual reinforcement, as their shared beliefs and assumptions remain unchallenged. Consequently, the lack of diversity stifles the generation of innovative ideas and prevents a comprehensive examination of potential risks and flaws in the group's decision-making process.

The Challenger space shuttle disaster on January 28, 1986, serves as a stark reminder of the dangers of groupthink within organizational contexts. As we examine the technicalities and decisions involved in this catastrophe, we unravel a complex web of factors, with groupthink at its heart.

The Challenger disaster stemmed from the failure of the O-rings, critical components of the shuttle's solid rocket boosters. Made of rubber, these rings sealed the booster segments' joints, preventing hot gasses from leaking and causing catastrophic structural failure. From the beginning of the shuttle program, engineers raised concerns about the O-rings' integrity, particularly in cold temperatures. Empirical evidence showed that the rings' elasticity decreased in colder environments, raising the risk of leaks.

On the eve of the ill-fated Challenger mission, temperature forecasts provoked debate among engineers and managers responsible for deciding whether to proceed with the launch. Some engineers adamantly expressed their concerns, arguing that the predicted temperatures were unprecedented, potentially placing the O-rings beyond their limits and risking disaster. Despite these voiced apprehensions, the launch decision remained unchanged.

Tragically, the Challenger space shuttle disintegrated just 73 seconds into its flight due to this flawed decision-making process. The accident claimed the lives of all seven crew members aboard.

The competitive environment at NASA during this time significantly contributed to conformance pressure. The space shuttle program aimed to instill national pride and demonstrate technological superiority. Falling behind schedule and facing funding challenges, those in the decision-making process found themselves under pressure to launch, regardless of doubts or lingering concerns. Additionally, the Challenger mission, which included the first teacher in space, Christa McAuliffe, was viewed as a public relations opportunity to gain support for NASA. This immense focus on meeting expectations and maintaining a positive image ultimately fostered an environment that amplified conformity while suppressing dissenting opinions.

Another factor contributing to conformity was the normalization of deviance, a term describing how repeated exposure to risky situations without negative consequences can cause individuals to accept these risks as standard. In the Challenger's case, previous shuttle launches experienced O-ring anomalies, but no major incidents resulted due to factors like warmer weather. As a result, though concerns were raised, management perceived the risks as tolerable, thereby undermining the urgency and severity of the engineers' apprehensions.

Undoubtedly, the pernicious effects of groupthink extend far beyond the confines of the Challenger disaster. In an environment where conformity is valorized, the voicing of dissenting opinions becomes fraught with perceived social risks, such as ostracism or ridicule. This fear of isolation may compel individuals to mask their dissenting views and adopt the prevailing ideas, regardless of the soundness of their own perspectives. As a result, alternative viewpoints and crucial critiques may never be presented, eliminating the opportunity for rigorous evaluation and debate.

8

Seeing only what is beautiful

A sunbeam stretches across a dreamy landscape, illuminating the golden halo surrounding the head of an angelic figure. Upon gazing at this ethereal vision, one cannot help but imbue the enshrouded figure with virtuous qualities. Such is the psychological foundation of the halo effect: a cognitive bias where one's perception of an individual's attributes and abilities is influenced, and often dramatically swayed, by a single charismatic trait.

Like the many other cognitive biases discussed, the halo effect resides in the way our brain processes information, preferring simplicity and coherence to the challenge of navigating a complex and nuanced world. As social beings striving for efficiency, we unconsciously formulate mental shortcuts to quickly infer broader characteristics from a single commendable feature. Unfortunately, this predisposition can deceive us into forming misjudgments, founded on the halo of a solitary attribute.

The term "halo effect" was first coined in 1920 by psychologist Edward Thorndike, who observed that soldiers were rated as intelligent, strong, and good-hearted based on their physical attractiveness alone. This observation has since spurred countless investigations into our psyche's intrinsic susceptibility to creating halos. Cognitive science has revealed that the halo effect transcends mere physical attractiveness; in fact, almost any praiseworthy trait—whether charisma, artistic talent, or wealth—can trigger our susceptibility to the halo effect.

While the halo effect is remarkably versatile, springing forth from a wide array of positive characteristics, certain traits wield a more potent influence in establishing these cognitive halos. Among the most potent is attractiveness, a quality demonstrated in Thorndike's observations among soldiers and in countless subsequent studies.

Psychologists have consistently found that people deemed physically attractive are perceived as more intelligent, empathetic, and competent in varied domains. A well-known study published in 1972 by University of Minnesota researchers found that attractive individuals were more likely to receive favorable treatment in legal scenarios, from both jurors and judges, in comparison to individuals deemed less attractive – a phenomenon they coined as the "beauty-is-good stereotype."

But attractiveness is by no means the sole arbiter of halos. The seminal work of Dr. Karen Dion highlighted the multifaceted dimensions of the halo effect and identified "peripheral cues," which she posited also contribute to the phenomenon. These peripheral cues encompass elements such as body language, eloquence, clothing, and contextual factors that have the potential to sway and influence our perception of a person's or institution's overall competence.

A notable example from Dr. Dion's research involved manipulating the attire of presenters during public talks on various subjects. Results illustrated that audience members were more likely to deem the information valid and trustworthy when the speakers were dressed professionally, as opposed to a casual or less refined style, highlighting the capacity of these peripheral cues to envelop our judgment in an illusory grasp.

These findings are particularly significant when we consider the implications it has for hiring and promotion decisions. Our judgment of a candidate's capabilities could be distorted if he or she simply looks the part or presents themselves well. This influence is even more problematic in situations where jobs require a high level of expertise and decision-making ability—instances where a charming appearance and a polished set of social skills may be of far less importance than analytical acuity or experience.

Yet, it is worth noting that the halo effect reaches beyond the individual level, unfolding with a rippling influence across societal constructs. For instance, the halo effect finds expression in revered institutions and organizations, bestowing them with an aura of excellence that may not necessarily align with the quality of their services. Whether it be renowned educational establishments, famed corporations, or admired sports teams, our susceptibility to constructing halos from broader sources remains astonishingly intact.

In recent history, few tales exemplify the halo effect's power and danger on a staggering scale as that of Elizabeth Holmes and Theranos. At its height, Theranos – a biotechnology start-up founded by Holmes – was championed as a revolutionary player in the diagnostics industry. With the promise of a revolutionary blood-testing technology that used only a fraction of the volume usually required by traditional tests, Theranos was poised to transform healthcare as we knew it. Elizabeth Holmes, CEO and visionary extraordinaire, had become one of the youngest self-made female billionaires in the world.

Holmes was anything but ordinary: her sleek black turtlenecks, deep voice, and unwavering stare became her calling card—a poised presence that evoked confidence and magnetism. A dazzling narrative formed around her, imbuing her with qualities such as genius, ambition, and fearlessness. And with that narrative, those who encountered and worked with her seemed all too eager to suspend disbelief in the face of mounting evidence that Theranos' core technology, the Edison, simply did not work.

The notion that a wunderkind and her revolutionary technology could upend the healthcare industry had proven too tantalizing to resist. Investors, medical professionals, and the media were all swept up in the captivating story of Elizabeth Holmes, and in doing so, overlooked the contradictions and inconsistencies emerging from behind the scenes. One specific instance that highlights the troubling extent to which critical thinking was discarded in favor of the halo effect was during a live demonstration of the Edison device.

In 2014, during a period when concerns about Theranos' technology were growing, Holmes was invited to present a live demonstration of the Edison device at a TEDMED event. In front of technologists, healthcare experts, and investors, she revealed the revolutionary device, praised its potential, and announced Theranos' partnership with Walgreens. Astoundingly, regardless of concerns raised by many in the field, including seasoned scientists, that such groundbreaking technology should have been rigorously scrutinized and tested by the medical community, the audience's response was overwhelmingly positive. Holmes' charisma, carefully cultivated image, and her company's lofty goals shielded her from the critical scrutiny one might expect from a room filled with experts.

This instance represents the chilling power of the halo effect at play: with a carefully crafted persona, Holmes ensnared the belief and trust of not only experts but also the general public, paving Theranos' path towards an eventual downfall that would cost investors nearly a billion dollars and leave countless patients with erroneous medical diagnoses.

The story of Elizabeth Holmes and Theranos serves as a haunting reminder that as long as we remain susceptible to the influence of the halo effect, we risk enshrining and empowering individuals who have not earned our admiration and trust on the basis of merit and accomplishment. As potent as first impressions may be, they should not eclipse the importance of corroborating evidence to make informed decisions in business, healthcare, and beyond. The stakes are too high, the consequences too devastating, for us to remain captive to the allure of the halo effect.

9

How ignorance blinds

We have explored how the halo effect perpetuates a cascade of misguided actions by venerating unproven heroes. Yet, on the other end of this spectrum is an equally delicate paradox, one that traps unwitting individuals in an illusion of their own grandeur.

We often assume that those who are brilliantly skilled and knowledgeable in a certain field must be well aware of their abilities, and that the incompetent would naturally realize their shortcomings. However, what if I told you that the incompetent often fail to recognize their own incompetence? Enter the Dunning-Kruger effect.

The Dunning-Kruger effect is a cognitive bias that leads unskilled individuals to inaccurately overestimate their own abilities. This psychological quirk not only undermines their capacity for self-assessment, but also prevents them from recognizing the extent of their incompetence. Remarkably, it means that the more incompetent people are, the less they seem to be aware of it.

To understand the Dunning-Kruger effect is to delve into an unnerving paradox of confidence and incompetence. The phenomenon was first described by social psychologists David Dunning and Justin Kruger in their seminal 1999 study and can be summarized as a cognitive distortion that leads those with limited knowledge or skill in a given domain to paradoxically overestimate their abilities. Conversely, the truly competent are prone to undervaluing their abilities, mistakenly assuming that tasks they find straightforward must be similarly so for others. In a cruel twist, the incompetent and overconfident are often incapable of recognizing their inadequacies, while the competent and modest stagnate in a sea of self-doubt.

But what illuminates the origin of this effect? Dunning and Kruger propose that the phenomenon arises as a direct outcome of our cognitive limitations. As humans, we possess a finite pool of cognitive resources, which are often taxed by the demands of learning any complex skill. In an attempt to reconcile these resource limitations, our cognitive system employs heuristic shortcuts to evaluate our abilities. The less skilled we are in a given area, the fewer benchmarks we possess to make accurate self-assessments; consequently, our cognitive system steps in to construct a false belief, compensating for a lack of understanding in that domain.

In 1995, the city of Pittsburgh was shaken by two brazen bank robberies committed by a man who made little effort to conceal his identity. This peculiar criminal was 44-year-old McArthur Wheeler, a man who genuinely believed he had unlocked the secret to becoming invisible. His method? Smearing his face with lemon juice.

Wheeler's misplaced confidence stemmed from a misunderstanding of a particular fact: that lemon juice could be used as an invisible ink. When heated, lemon juice turns visible, revealing hidden messages. Wheeler mistakenly inferred that by applying lemon juice to his face, he would be rendered invisible to surveillance cameras.

On that fateful day, Wheeler confidently strode into two Pittsburgh banks, face covered with lemon juice. He even paused to smile and wave at one of the security cameras. Later that day, he was featured on the local news as the unidentified bank robber. Wheeler was subsequently identified by the police, thanks to several acquaintances who recognized his face.

McArthur Wheeler was not simply a man who failed to recognize that he didn't possess the necessary skills to pull off a successful bank heist; rather, he was so ignorant of his own ignorance that he naively put his belief in an absurd plan. His misplaced confidence, combined with his lack of understanding and self-awareness, not only led to the eventual failure of his criminal aspirations, but also to his capture and arrest.

When we consider the case of McArthur Wheeler, it begs the question: How does what we know—or rather, what we don't know—shape our self-perception? This knot of knowledge, confidence, and self-awareness twists and turns through the human experience like the branches of an ancient tree, revealing surprising insights along the way.

In their groundbreaking research, David Dunning and Justin Kruger discovered that as we gain expertise in a subject, our confidence grows—for a time. We feel an initial sense of mastery when we first comprehend the basics, where our lack of nuance in the subject leads to an inflated view of our capabilities.

This honeymoon period of learning is short-lived, however. As we delve deeper, burrowing into the subject's complexities and intricacies, the scope of our ignorance becomes glaringly apparent. Our confidence plummets as we realize how much more there is to learn, and the vast chasms of missed opportunities and incomprehensible facts lie open before us. This stage is crucial, as it is here that the divide between the truly dedicated and those who shy away from the challenge becomes apparent.

Those who endure this period of intellectual discomfort, leaning into the uncertainty, find that they gradually build a more nuanced understanding of the subject. As this process unfolds, the strong interplay between knowledge and self-awareness becomes increasingly clear. Paradoxically, we come to recognize that the more we know, the more we become aware of the extent of our ignorance. This insight fosters intellectual humility—the ability to ground our confidence in the reality of our expertise and a measured recognition of the limits of our knowledge.

Yet, it is important to remember that true confidence does not mean we remain shackled by the weight of our shortcomings. Instead, it allows us to embrace the pockets of our expertise and gives us the courage to admit when we are less informed. This marriage of competence and humility is the cornerstone of a strong self-awareness, one that navigates the murky currents of human knowledge with grace and agility.

For those who squander their intellectual appetite, acquiescing to the allure of unfounded confidence, an entirely different narrative unfolds—one characterized by a woeful failure of self-awareness, the perilous overestimation of one's abilities, and a blindness to the remedial effects of learning and growth.

To better appreciate the subtle dance of knowledge, confidence, and self-awareness, let us turn our attention to a domain that has captured the imagination of millions: the enigmatic world of the stock market. From illustrious empires to everyday individuals, fortunes rise and fall on the whims of the market, and yet, a curious phenomenon plays out on its unpredictable stage, a manifestation of the Dunning-Kruger effect in action.

Consider John, an aspiring investor who has recently immersed himself in books, blogs, and podcasts on the subject. Armed with his newfound knowledge, he ventures into the stock market with eagerness, confident that his research has endowed him with the acumen to make savvy investment decisions. However, the truth of the matter is that John stands at the precipice of overconfidence: His superficial understanding of the field has laid the groundwork for a distorted sense of self-assurance.

John's adventure begins with a string of successful investments, each one boosting his confidence, feeding his belief in his investing prowess. However, as the fickle winds change, his luck takes a turn. With the market swinging wildly, he scrambles to secure his gains, unwittingly engaging in a series of misinformed decisions. In the end, John's portfolio suffers, his confidence deflates, and he falls prey to one of the most deceptive pitfalls of all: the illusion of control.

The tale of John may seem a caricature, but in reality, it is all too familiar. The Dunning-Kruger effect thrives in the vast and complex landscape of the stock market, where amateur investors frequently overestimate their proficiency. Seemingly tantalized by the prospect of wealth and success, they look past the expertise of seasoned professionals and instead, place their trust in their fragile foundation of knowledge. The allure of mastering the stock market blinds them not just to its inherent unpredictability but, more significantly, to the awareness that their own competence is but a single grain of sand on a vast, uncharted beach.

In this high-stakes arena, the interplay between knowledge, confidence, and self-awareness is on full display. The meteoric rise of one's portfolio may spring from sheer luck rather than a mastery of the market, yet it is all too easy for an amateur investor like John to misattribute the cause. When such individuals cling to their untested theories or novice strategies, they create a perfect storm of cognitive distortions, setting the stage for the inevitable fall.

10

Overlooking circumstances

In unraveling the complexities of human behavior, it is important to appreciate that the ways in which we perceive others can be profoundly shaped by our cognitive biases. One such bias, the fundamental attribution error, holds the key to understanding a multitude of misjudgments we make about others—often without even realizing it.

The fundamental attribution error refers to the cognitive tendency to overemphasize the role of a person's character or disposition, at the expense of adequately considering the contextual factors that may be at play. In other words, we instinctively default to attributing a person's actions or behavior to their inherent personality traits, without sufficiently acknowledging the circumstances that might have influenced their behavior.

Imagine, for a moment, that you are on your daily commute to work, and you happen to witness an altercation between a driver and a pedestrian. The pedestrian, crossing in haste, appears to have ventured onto the road when the signal was still red. You might be tempted to label the pedestrian as reckless, thoughtless, or even selfish—all characteristics that suggest traits inherent to their personality. However, in formulating this judgment, you may neglect to consider external factors that could have contributed to the pedestrian's behavior, such as an urgent appointment, a family emergency, or even an honest misperception of the traffic signal.

The essence of the fundamental attribution error lies in our propensity to leap to conclusions about others' character, while disregarding possible situational influences. This cognitive bias operates subtly, seeping into our judgments almost imperceptibly and shaping our perceptions of those around us. Though it may, at times, seem innocuous, the implications of the fundamental attribution error—particularly when it infiltrates our political, legal, and social systems—are far-reaching and profound.

A striking manifestation of the fundamental attribution error can be found in the sentencing disparities between black and white offenders, which has been highlighted by numerous studies.

One such study, conducted by Rehavi and Starr (2014), entailed a comprehensive examination of federal criminal cases in the United States over a 6-year period. Their rigorous analysis revealed that black defendants were, on average, sentenced to prison terms 9% longer than white defendants who were convicted of similar crimes. This disparity persisted even after controlling for a variety of mitigating factors, such as the severity of the crime, the defendant's criminal history, and the judge's characteristics.

How, then, does the fundamental attribution error contribute to these disparities in criminal sentencing? Research suggests that the attribution error may fuel racial bias in judges and juries, leading them to perceive black defendants as inherently more prone to criminal behavior. In doing so, their judgments may overemphasize the role of individual character, overlooking the broader socioeconomic and systemic factors that contribute to criminality.

For instance, the Eberhardt et al. (2006) experiment, "Looking Deathworthy: Perceived Stereotypicality of Black Defendants Predicts Capital-Sentencing

Outcomes," demonstrated the power of racial biases in shaping the judgments of mock jurors and serves as a compelling illustration of how the fundamental attribution error, in tandem with racial bias, can have profound consequences in the realm of criminal justice. The study provides valuable insights into the cognitive processes that underlie judicial decision-making and how they are compounded by perceptions of race.

The experiment was divided into two parts, each designed to analyze specific aspects of participants' judgments. In the first part of the study, Eberhardt and her colleagues sought to explore how perceived stereotypicality of black defendants influenced decisions in capital-sentencing cases. They compiled photographs of black and white male defendants who had been tried for murder in the state of Philadelphia between 1979 and 1999. They then asked white undergraduate students to rate the degree to which each defendant's appearance was stereotypically "black," using a 7-point scale ranging from "not at all" to "extremely."

Following this, the researchers examined the trial outcomes of these defendants, factoring in variables such as the defendant's attractiveness, the victim's race, and the quality of legal counsel. They discovered a striking pattern: black defendants who were perceived to be highly stereotypical in appearance were significantly more likely to receive the death penalty than those who appeared less stereotypical.

In the second part of the experiment, Eberhardt shifted the focus to another group of participants—black and white mock jurors. The participants were presented with a fictional case involving a black or white defendant accused of a violent crime. The defendant's photograph was doctored to appear either more or less stereotypically black, by digitally altering the nose and lip size. Importantly, the defendant's race was not mentioned in the case description.

During their deliberations, the researchers measured the participants' tendency to make both internal (i.e., dispositional) and external (i.e., situational) attributions for the defendant's alleged behavior. Remarkably, the results showed that when the defendant appeared more stereotypically black, mock jurors were significantly more likely to make internal attributions, regardless of the actual race of the defendant.

The recognition of the interplay between the fundamental attribution error and racial bias in sentencing calls for a profound reflection on how our cognitive tendencies can exacerbate and perpetuate social inequalities. By scrutinizing the role played by cognitive biases in our criminal justice system, we create the opportunity to initiate meaningful reforms that promote a more equitable and just society.

The implications of the fundamental attribution error extend far beyond the courtroom, seeping into the fabric of our society and shaping how we perceive the world. It is crucial to recognize that the consequences of this pernicious cognitive bias are not confined to a select few, but rather permeate all strata of human interactions. We must become aware of how the error

At the core of the fundamental attribution error is the tendency to misjudge others based on a myopic perspective, rather than considering the underlying situational factors that play a role in behavior. In our day-to-day lives, this propensity can lead to miscommunication and misunderstanding between individuals, hampering the development of rapport and trust. Moreover, it engenders a toxic environment in which blame and personal attacks supplant empathy and constructive dialogue.

In organizational contexts, the attribution error can permeate work relation-ships and hinder the effectiveness of teamwork. When a co-worker fails to fulfill their responsibilities, it is all too easy to label them as "incompetent" or "lazy," ignoring their personal circumstances, such as family issues, health problems, or other external stressors. This lack of understanding can lead to the erosion of interpersonal bonds and induce the formation of cliques or factions.

The fundamental attribution error also inadvertently reinforces persisting social stereotypes, casting further obstacles in the path of marginalized groups. As previously illustrated, the attribution error can contribute to racial bias in sentencing and exacerbate societal divisions. Furthermore, it can bolster gender inequalities by attributing the underrepresentation of women in leadership positions to personal inadequacies—such as an alleged lack of ambition or assertiveness—rather than examining systemic barriers, such as discriminatory hiring practices or unconscious biases.

Similarly, when encountering a struggling homeless individual, we tend to ponder their lack of resourcefulness or moral character, rather than considering the complex interplay of social and economic forces that leave millions adrift in abject poverty. This mode of thinking, compounded by the attribution error, conceals the systemic issues that contribute to such disparities and thus hinders our capacity to devise effective solutions.

A profound understanding of the fundamental attribution error—its roots, manifestations, and ensuing consequences—creates an opportunity for us to expand our horizons and embrace the complexity inherent in human behavior. By doing so, we can begin to break free from the shackles of prejudice and build a society that nurtures understanding, empathy, and fairness.

11

The deceptive allure of "I knew it all along"

To properly address the phenomenon of hindsight bias, we must first define and understand its essence. Often colloquially referred to as the "I-knew-it-all-along" effect, hindsight bias is our well-documented tendency to inaccurately assume that we could have predicted an outcome, once we are made aware of the actual result. This cognitive bias skews our perception of the past, morphing it into a polished narrative in which events appear to have unfolded in a linear and logical fashion.

One may ask: how does hindsight bias emerge from the workings of the human mind? After all, isn't the capacity to anticipate and predict crucial to our survival and success? While foresight is indeed necessary for making informed decisions, hindsight bias poses a distinct and often deceptive challenge to our decision-making process. We commonly construct our mental models of the world in a cause-and-effect manner, attempting to derive patterns and connections from the myriad of variables that surround us. Consequently, we are naturally predisposed to seek coherence and order, even if it means unconsciously enhancing the predictability of past events.

At the heart of hindsight bias lies our innate need for control. By convincing ourselves that we "knew it all along," we manage to assuage the discomfort caused by uncertainty and maintain a semblance of mastery over our environment. Furthermore, hindsight bias supports the narrative of our personal competency and bolsters our self-esteem, as we like to see ourselves as shrewd observers who can easily deduce the trajectory of unfolding situations. This, in turn, leads to an illusory sense of confidence in our predictive abilities, while simultaneously neglecting the complex interplay of various factors that ultimately shape the outcome.

In order to further our understanding of hindsight bias, we must also explore the roles played by memory and cognitive processes in creating this cognitive distortion. Our memory is often perceived as a reliable storehouse for past events; however, the reality is that it is a malleable system continuously influenced and restructured by new experiences and information. This very plasticity of our memory serves as a fertile ground for hindsight bias to take root and flourish.

Three key processes contribute to the development of hindsight bias: memory distortion, outcome knowledge, and cognitive reconstruction. As our memory navigates the ever-shifting landscape of recollections, our perception of past beliefs and predictions can become malleable. In fact, we might even reinterpret or selectively forget certain aspects that don't align with the outcome, ultimately settling for an edited version of the past.

When exposed to new information—the outcome, in this context—it becomes challenging to recall the level of uncertainty we originally experienced during the decision-making process. Our brains are quick to accommodate the outcome knowledge by retroactively rationalizing and adjusting our initial predictions. The result is an overestimation of the congruence between our original beliefs and the subsequent outcome, fueling the conviction that we "knew it all along."

Cognitive reconstruction is another potent driver of hindsight bias. As we process new, outcome-related information, we instinctively generate plausible explanations and weave a coherent narrative. Unbeknownst to us, those rationalizations serve to alter our memory, making the events appear more predictable and the connections between variables more evident.

The potency of these cognitive processes renders our memory and perception vulnerable to hindsight bias. The dynamic interplay between mnemonic and cognitive factors shapes our retroactive interpretation of the past, often fooling us into believing that we foresaw the outcome all along.

In the realm of entrepreneurship, we encounter a tangible manifestation of hindsight bias. The world of startups, filled with risk, uncertainty, and the thrill of chasing dreams, provides fertile ground for this cognitive distortion to thrive. Entrepreneurs stake their visions, resources, and convictions on their ability to innovate and disrupt the market. However, despite exhibiting exceptional determination and resilience, entrepreneurs are found to be highly susceptible to this bias, often underestimating their initial optimism and overvaluing their predictive prowess.

One illuminating study by Gavan Cassar underscores the pervasiveness of hindsight bias in the entrepreneurial domain. Cassar's analysis of 705 entrepreneurs from failed startups revealed some striking insights into the power of this cognitive quirk. Prior to their ventures' collapse, approximately 77.3% of these entrepreneurs wholeheartedly believed that their startups were bound for success. Yet, in the aftermath of failure, only 58% conceded that they had initially held such optimistic views.

This distortion in entrepreneurs' recollection of their earlier beliefs demonstrates the nature of hindsight bias. After experiencing a setback, their memory becomes malleable in light of the new outcome knowledge, skewing their perception of their past mindset. Post-failure reflections on their entrepreneurial journeys revealed that many participants unconsciously downplayed the extent of their former optimism, while retroactively inflating their perceived foresight.

The implications of hindsight bias are particularly profound in the world of entrepreneurship. Entrepreneurs who fall prey to this bias risk becoming overly confident in their ability to accurately predict the outcomes of future ventures. This inflated perception of their prognostic skills can then lead them to unrealistically overestimate the likelihood of success in subsequent ventures. As a result, hindsight bias doesn't only distort entrepreneurs' recall of the past but has the potential to misguide their future decision-making, by feeding into a cycle of overconfidence, and inadequately assessing risks and challenges that lie ahead.

In fact, hindsight bias has a firm grasp on all our daily lives, coloring our interpretations of various events and fostering a false sense of certainty that we "knew it all along." From politics and sports to market trends and interpersonal dynamics, hindsight bias pervades various dimensions of our existence, subtly reshaping our understanding of unfolding events.

In the realm of politics, hindsight bias often emerges after electoral outcomes. As the results roll in and the winners emerge, numerous observers are struck by the belief that they anticipated the outcome with marked accuracy. Newspapers and commentators are filled with retrospective wisdom about the crucial factors that determined the election: economic conditions, the candidates' charisma, or unique campaign strategies. Often, these new "inevitable" narratives shadow more complex precursors, a rich confluence of variables that made the probabilities far more uncertain than they now appear in hindsight.

The vicissitudes of financial markets offer further examples of hindsight bias at work. As market forces fluctuate, analysts and investors, armed with the knowledge of the recent market shifts, perceive these complex changes as foreseeable and predictable. This delusion of predictability feeds the illusion that investment decisions could have been optimized had they just relied on their "knowledge" that the stocks were bound to rise or fall when they did. In truth, the uncertainty and volatility that permeate financial markets make predicting such shifts a Herculean task.

Lastly, hindsight bias also shapes our social interactions. Upon learning that a friend's relationship has ended, we might catch ourselves recounting the various red flags that had allegedly indicated their incompatibility all along: their divergent interests, opposing life goals, or distinct communication styles. In such instances, hindsight bias constructs a neat narrative, selectively highlighting the clues that seem to align with an outcome that was far less predictable than our memory now suggests.

12

Our tribal tendencies

In-group bias refers to the natural human tendency to favor those who belong to our own social groups over those relegated to the "out-groups." This psychological predisposition influences the way we perceive, evaluate, and treat individuals based on the arbitrary demarcations made between "us" and "them." Its manifestation can span across various dimensions, including race, religion, nationality, socio-economic status, and even affiliations with sports teams or political parties.

This deeply-rooted phenomenon finds its origin in our evolutionary history. As early humans formed communities to survive the harsh conditions of prehistoric life, the distinction between in-group members and outsiders became a functional tool for resource allocation and self-preservation. In other words, forming social bonds and cooperating exclusively with in-group members served as an adaptive strategy essential for survival and reproduction.

However, the contemporary landscape, characterized by rapid globalization and interdependence among diverse communities, has blurred the once-crucial boundaries between in-group and out-group members. Despite this progress, in-group bias continues to influence our decision-making and behavior, fueled by psychological mechanisms such as self-enhancement, social identity, and mental shortcuts.

Self-enhancement refers to the human propensity to maintain a positive self-image, which can be achieved through favorable evaluations of one's own social group. By perceiving our group as superior, we elevate our sense of self-worth and maintain a positive self-esteem. This inclination towards self-enhancement drives in-group bias, as it entrenches a hierarchical order that invites us to disregard the value of out-group members.

Furthermore, social identity theory posits that our self-concept is highly intertwined with the groups we associate with, and it compels us to maximize the distinction between our own group and others. This process of accentuating differences not only solidifies our sense of belonging but also strengthens the allure of group loyalty.

Various factors can contribute to the development of in-group bias, ranging from individual experiences to cultural influences and cognitive shortcuts. Exploring these factors allows us to better understand the complexity of this pervasive psychological mechanism and how it emerges in different contexts.

One factor that contributes to in-group bias is the process of socialization, which begins in childhood. As we grow up, we learn patterns of thought and behavior from the immediate environments we inhabit, such as our families, schools, and local communities. When these environments display a preference for the in-group, such attitudes become engrained in our developing minds, rendering us particularly susceptible to in-group favoritism as we encounter new situations and individuals.

Moreover, societal norms and values play a significant role in reinforcing in-group bias. Mass media, formal education, and popular culture often reinforce and perpetuate stereotypes and expectations of certain social groups, leading to the reinforcement of in-group bias among the general population. In this manner, cultural forces can mold the ways in which we evaluate and relate to others based on group membership.

Another factor that contributes to the development of in-group bias is the tendency to seek cognitive coherence and simplicity. Humans inherently prefer thoughts and beliefs that are consistent with their existing mental framework. Consequently, when confronted with information that challenges the status quo or the established order of social groups, we may internalize this information selectively or reinterpret it to fit our existing schema, thereby solidifying our in-group bias.

Finally, a key contributor to in-group bias is our reliance on cognitive heuristics or mental shortcuts. In order to navigate the complexities of human interaction, we rely on heuristics, simple and efficient decision-making strategies that facilitate rapid judgments. For instance, using the categorization of people into social groups as a heuristic can simplify the perception of others by organizing people into familiar clusters. However, this mental shortcut often comes at the expense of nuance and individuality, as it can lead to sweeping generalizations and reinforce in-group bias.

One of the most compelling demonstrations of the development of in-group bias can be seen in the famous Robbers Cave experiment, conducted by social psychologist Muzafer Sherif and his colleagues in the 1950s. This groundbreaking study revealed how artificial group divisions can give rise to in-group favoritism and intergroup hostility, even in the absence of pre-existing biases or conflicts.

Prior to the initiation of the study, Sherif and his team carefully selected 22 boys who showed no indications of enmity toward one another. These twelve-year-olds, who were all from comparable backgrounds regarding educational and socioeconomic status, were brought to a remote location in Oklahoma's Robbers Cave State Park. Upon their arrival at the campsite, they were randomly divided into two groups – the Eagles and the Rattlers.

Sherif's team meticulously crafted separate living areas for each group and introduced them to their surroundings without any knowledge of the other group's existence. The researchers, disguised as camp personnel, took positions as counselors and supervisors within each group to carefully observe the development of group identification. With the stage set, the researchers shifted their focus to promoting cohesion within each group.

To cultivate group unity, the camp coordinators orchestrated various activities that required teamwork, such as swimming, hiking, and problem-solving tasks. As the boys worked collectively towards a common goal, they formed strong bonds with one another, developing a sense of comradeship. Each group spontaneously created its own identity, complete with coined nicknames, group flags, unique rituals, and even elected a leader that they collectively respected.

Once the researchers deemed that both groups had achieved sufficient internal cohesion, they orchestrated a seemingly accidental encounter between the Eagles and the Rattlers, marking the beginning of intergroup competition. A series of contests began, boasting a shared prize that only the winning team could claim.

As the competition became fiercer, the boys' in-group identification intensified, pushing them to favor their group members and exhibit prejudice against the rival group. The in-group bias manifested in various forms, from name-calling and verbal insults to demeaning the rivals' abilities or achievements. The euphoria of a victory only heightened the in-group's sense of moral superiority, further reinforcing in-group bias.

Recognizing the magnitude of the artificially induced conflict, Sherif moved towards the last phase of the experiment – alleviating existing hostility and promoting collaboration. The researchers created situations in which both groups had to cooperatively endeavor to solve problems, like fixing a shared water source they depended on. As they worked together to achieve a common goal, their animosity began to dissipate, illustrating that under the right circumstances, intergroup differences could be bridged.

In a nutshell, the Robbers Cave experiment vividly demonstrated the strength of group identification, how it can develop under certain conditions, and the potential for intergroup hostility when the groups are pitted against each other. Its revelation of how even arbitrary boundaries can spark major divisions reminds us to be mindful of how our own group affiliations can spark potential biases.

13

Why we flaunt our successes and excuse our failures

Following our exploration of in-group bias, we now turn our attention to another pervasive cognitive bias that affects individuals across various spheres of life: the self-serving bias. This phenomenon has a profound impact on how we perceive ourselves, often enhancing our self-esteem by distorting our perceptions of reality.

At its core, the self-serving bias refers to our tendency to attribute our successes to internal factors, such as our skills, abilities, and hard work, while blaming our failures on external circumstances, such as bad luck or situational constraints. This cognitive bias acts as a self-protective mechanism that allows us to maintain a positive self-image and preserves our self-esteem in the face of adversity.

One of the reasons behind the manifestation of self-serving bias lies in our innate need for self-enhancement. Humans possess a deep-seated desire to view themselves in a positive light, which in turn drives our inclination to interpret information in a manner that bolsters our self-esteem. For instance, if we perform well in a test, we are likely to believe that our hard work and intelligence were the primary factors contributing to our success, while downplaying the role of luck or other external factors.

On the other hand, if we perform poorly, it is more convenient for our self-esteem to blame external forces, rather than question our abilities or efforts. This selective attribution helps to shield our self-image from the potentially harmful effects of failure, reducing the cognitive dissonance that may arise when our performance does not align with our expectations or self-perception.

Furthermore, this biased attribution may be exacerbated by the relative lack of objective criteria for assessing one's own performance and abilities. We often rely on self-assessment to gauge our skills or the success of our endeavors, which can be influenced by our desire to see ourselves in a positive light, further reinforcing the self-serving bias.

As we delve further into the relationship between self-serving bias and self-esteem, it becomes apparent that the two phenomena are intricately intertwined, each one both influencing and being influenced by the other.

At the heart of the interplay between self-serving bias and self-esteem lies the fundamental need for self-preservation. Preserving a stable and favorable self-image is crucial for maintaining mental health, as it enables us to cope with the uncertainties and challenges that life presents. This self-preservation, however, often comes at the expense of an accurate and unbiased understanding of ourselves, leading us to succumb to the allure of the self-serving bias.

When our self-esteem is high, we are more likely to exhibit the self-serving bias, as it resonates with our pre-existing beliefs about our abilities and worth. Under these circumstances, the self-serving bias often operates in a self-sustaining manner, feeding into our sense of self-worth and reinforcing our positive image of ourselves. Within this context, the self-serving bias serves as a means to maintain our already high self-esteem, enabling us to bounce back from setbacks and persevere in the face of adversity.

However, the relationship between the self-serving bias and self-esteem is not always positive. For individuals with low self-esteem, the self-serving bias may be less prominent or even operate in reverse, leading them to attribute their successes to external factors (such as luck) and their failures to internal factors (such as a lack of ability). This maladaptive form of the self-serving bias, which is sometimes referred to as the "self-defeating" or "self-destructive" bias, can perpetuate a cycle of negative self-image and further erode self-esteem.

The world of sports, with its emphasis on achievement and personal prowess, provides fertile ground for the manifestation of the self-serving bias. Athletes often have a tendency to credit their successes to their hard work and natural talent while deflecting blame for failures onto factors beyond their control.

A notable example of this phenomenon can be observed in the 2018 US Open final where Serena Williams faced off against Naomi Osaka. Early on, Williams received several coaching violations from umpire Carlos Ramos, which ultimately culminated in her being penalized a full game. After exchanging heated words with Ramos during the match, Williams famously accused him of sexism after it had concluded, stating it was unfair because male players get away with similar or worse behavior without punishment.

However, an examination of both sideline coaching rules as well as specific actions leading up to the penalties portrays that Williams' behavior may exemplify self-serving bias. As per tennis rules, players cannot receive direct guidance or strategy support from their coaches during matches; yet despite being caught receiving hand signals from her coach Patrick Mouratoglou (who later admitted his actions), she maintained that "I don't cheat to win." Moreover, Williams smashed her racket out of frustration and vocally confronted Ramos even after repeated verbal warnings—a set pattern for violation penalties dictated by tennis rules regardless of gender.

Rather than conceding that she violated these rules (which all players must adhere to) and acknowledging responsibility for her actions contributing to her loss—including taking into account how emotions may have negatively impacted performance beyond the penalties—Williams partially blamed external factors like sexism for her defeat in front of millions watching globally.

This incident illustrates how our need to maintain a positive self-concept can exaggerate an athlete's perception about their personal agency influencing outcomes—leading them down the road towards biased judgments about their skill and luck versus rule adherence or behavior. By ascribing the events that transpired to sexism, Williams potentially engaged in self-serving bias to protect her identity as a high-performing and virtuous athlete.

Moving from the realm of sports to the domain of politics, self-serving bias can be found operating at the heart of political partisanship and the process of attributing blame for adverse events or outcomes. As individuals are naturally inclined to maintain a positive view of themselves—including the beliefs and values they hold—it comes as no surprise that cognitive biases would influence one's perception of political parties, figures, and policies with which one aligns.

Political partisanship often enables individuals to attribute successes or desirable outcomes to their own party's hard work, virtuous motives, and intelligent ideologies while dismissing their failures as having originated due to factors beyond their control, such as sabotage by opponents or unfair media coverage. Conversely, when assessing an opposing party's achievements or failings, adherents look past situational explanations; instead, crediting luck if successful or easily grasping onto evidence that confirms preconceived notions about their inherently faulty ideologies or corrupt leadership if unsuccessful.

A vivid illustration from recent times took place during the 2020 U.S. presidential election amidst debates regarding voting irregularities impacting the outcome—where self-serving bias played a crucial role in interpreting available evidence (or lack thereof). Certain factions supporting then-President Donald Trump were quick to disregard exhaustive investigations finding no persuasive evidence to substantiate allegations of widespread voter fraud; these individuals sometimes engaged in selective skepticism rejecting contradictory accounts while believing far-reaching conspiratorial theories that painted opponents as sinister powers thwarting electoral processes.

Similarly, opposing factions ascribed former President Trump's 2016 victory partly to Russian interference despite extensive probes demonstrating it wielded minimal actual impact on election results—while downplaying internal Democratic campaign failures.

Notably harming healthy public discourse on vital issues by promoting an "us vs them" mentality where external circumstances are either magnified (for negative outcomes) or minimized (for positive ones), self-serving bias within political partisanship fosters a culture of attributing blame and avoiding responsibility. In extreme cases, it can drive forward more polarized societies fueled by mistrust and ignorance, where discord overshadows facts or reason, ultimately precluding efficient resolution of disputes.

14

The misguided assumption of our influence

As we continue our exploration of cognitive biases, we arrive at the compelling concept of the illusion of control, which has widespread implications and can shape our perspectives in various contexts. The illusion of control refers to the tendency for individuals to overestimate their ability to influence events or achieve desired outcomes, despite facing limitations or external factors that are inherently beyond their grasp.

Psychologist Ellen Langer first identified this phenomenon in a series of experiments conducted in the 1970s. Her research demonstrated that participants often displayed an inflated sense of personal agency when presented with situations involving elements entirely driven by chance or uncontrollable factors, like predicting coin flips or lottery numbers. Intriguingly, this overconfidence emerged even more prominently in scenarios where people perceived there to be some connection between their actions and outcomes—such as when given imagined "skills" or "strategies" for predicting random occurrences—despite these being purely illusory constructs.

So why does the illusion of control take root so easily within human cognition? At its core lies an inherent need for individuals to seek order, predictability, and a sense of security in an often unpredictable world. By believing they have direct influence over their environment or future outcomes, people can feel a heightened level of mastery and reduce anxiety stemming from uncertainty.

The availability heuristic (discussed earlier) also contributes significantly toward reinforcing the illusion of control: Individuals might focus on previous instances where they believed they had succeeded in exerting authority over a situation—even if it was by pure coincidence—while ignoring other moments where their attempts did not yield predicted results. This selective attention consolidates a biased mental model promoting enhanced self-sufficiency and fostering distorted views about one's true impact on a given situation.

As we delve deeper into the factors that contribute to the development of our irrational belief in control, we find a fascinating interplay between psychological tendencies, individual experiences, and situational aspects.

Firstly, the desire for agency influences how susceptible one is to this illusion. Human beings crave a sense of autonomy and are hardwired to seek meaning in their existence. Feelings of powerlessness or helplessness can be quite distressing; as such, an inflated belief in personal influence acts as a self-preservatory mechanism in navigating unstable or unfamiliar environments. By asserting control over external variables, individuals gain comfort from their perceived abilities to shape reality according to their whims.

Secondly, cognitive influences stemming from other biases play a significant role in reinforcing illusory control. As previously mentioned, availability heuristic primes us towards remembering instances that support our beliefs while ignoring contradicting evidence—a tendency that feeds directly into maintaining illusory control fantasies. Furthermore, recency bias amplifies these impressions by prioritizing recent examples where we have exerted apparent influence on outcomes, further solidifying subjective notions of effective control.

Another factor involves personal experiences that accompany prior successes or positive events. When an individual encounters accomplishments either due to coincidences or genuine skillful performances, they may come to associate these with controllable aspects within unrelated circumstances later on—a cognition fueled primarily by hindsight bias, as discussed earlier.

Additionally, social and cultural effects contribute significantly toward shaping individuals' convictions about their levels of authority over various phenomena. For example, confidence-building measures used within educational settings—like encouraging students to develop problem-solving skills—manufacture environments where pupils cultivate faith in their faculties for conquering complex issues beyond their scope. While this may effectively groom learners for challenges they encounter academically or professionally later on, it can inadvertently spawn stubborn illusions about one's omnipotence across myriad spheres.

Lastly, situational factors may further inflate the illusion of control. Introducing even the slightest degree of skill-centric context, like allowing participants to select lottery numbers in an experiment, seems to trick our subconscious into thinking these arbitrary decisions translate into control over ensuing results purely based on randomness.

Now let's turn our attention to a more subtle yet pervasive example of the illusion of control in daily life—our obsession with vitamin supplements. The health and wellness industry is rife with promises of enhanced vitality, increased energy, and even lengthened lifespans that can be achieved simply by consuming the "right" combination of vitamins, minerals, and other purportedly essential nutrients.

As conscientious consumers, we may logically understand that practicing a balanced diet, regular exercise, and adopting healthy habits contribute significantly to overall wellness—yet this knowledge does not hinder the allure of ingesting supplements as secret weapons against illness or infirmity. Consequently, an overwhelming majority ventures into pharmacies and supermarket aisles stocking up on colorful capsules and tablets designed to fill presumed dietary gaps or provide additional benefits unattainable through food alone.

Our vulnerability to the illusion of control propels us to selectively embrace information confirming our desire for shortcuts in health maintenance. Subjected to constant bombardment by advertisements showcasing fit individuals attributing success in part to various products—alongside scientific-sounding jargon substantiating impressive claims—we come tantalizingly close to surrendering agency over our wellbeing too easily.

Of course, many credible studies have confirmed the benefits of taking specific vitamins under particular circumstances, such as prescribed supplementation for diagnosed deficiencies. However, these cases are quite different from the general endorsement of widespread and indiscriminate consumption. Such consumption is often based on misguided beliefs about personal mastery and seamless integration with marketed lifestyles that promise easy enhancements.

Ultimately, falling prey to the illusionary control within the realm of personal health means focusing excessively on superficial actions with minimal impacts rather than allocating time and resources towards establishing genuinely beneficial habits like adopting nutrient-rich diets or exercising consistently. A failure to recognize these priorities often results in considerable lopsidedness concerning individual approaches; thus perpetuating unrealistic expectations about supplementary input as the sole determinant of personal success in preserving health, potentially leading to disappointment and confounded decision-making.

15

The battle of conflicting beliefs

As we progress through our exploration of human intelligence and its dualistic manifestations, we now arrive at the intriguing and perplexing psychological phenomenon of cognitive dissonance. Before delving into its far-reaching implications and repercussions on human decision-making, it is essential to establish a clear understanding of this concept.

Cognitive dissonance refers to the mental discomfort that arises from holding two or more conflicting beliefs, attitudes, or values. This unease often manifests as emotional tension, driving individuals to seek resolutions for inconsistencies within their internal constructs. After all, humans have an innate desire for psychological coherence—to weave life's disparate threads into a consistent tapestry reflecting their understanding of the world.

Discovered by psychologist Leon Festinger in the 1950s, this concept has since been instrumental in deciphering many aspects of human behavior central to personal choices made without complete information. The theory posits that when faced with dissonant cognitions—such as simultaneously perceiving smoking as harmful while being a smoker—one strives towards consonance through various means: altering either the conflicting belief or justifying actions contrary to ideals.

This reconciliation process typically unfolds in one of three ways: changing a previously held belief (e.g., convincing oneself smoking isn't that harmful), seeking new information supporting existing thoughts (e.g., researching supposed benefits of smoking), or altering current behaviors (e.g., quitting smoking). Any action intended to lessen cognitive dissonance's discomfort propels individuals toward rationalizations necessary for maintaining cherished convictions and worldviews.

The unsettling sensation that accompanies cognitive dissonance is not merely an intellectual exercise—it has a visceral impact on our emotional state and well-being. This discomfort may appear subtle at first, like an itch we cannot quite pinpoint but gradually builds into an unbearable annoyance gnawing away at our sense of equilibrium.

Curiously, our resistance to the tensions created by discordant thoughts illustrates a fundamental aspect of human nature: the tension between personal self-preservation and truth-seeking instincts. We might think that coming across new information conflicting with our established opinions would spark curiosity and stimulate an objective reevaluation process. However, more often than not, this mental feedback loop drives us in the opposite direction—forcing us to dig in our heels and reject competing ideas as threats to cherished narratives sustaining our identity.

This emotional aversion to cognitive dissonance spills over multiple facets of our lives—from relationships, politics, religion to matters seemingly trivial—for example is your favorite dish genuinely enjoyable or it endures as a sentimental relic tracing back to nostalgic memories?

Drawing upon two primary sources—the integration of social norms acquired from family upbringing and societal influences along with personal experiences shaping individual worldviews—we craft sophisticated intellectual defenses against anything creating cognitive dissonance. It leads us along twisted routes where upholding internal consistency becomes paramount—casting doubt on objective evidence regardless of its significance.

Our ability to recognize cognitive dissonance dates back centuries, even if the term itself seems relatively modern. The ancient Greek storyteller Aesop masterfully showcased the universality of this human quirk in one of his most famous fables, "The Fox and the Grapes."

As we step inside this allegorical tale, picture a fox wandering through a lush forest on one fine summer day. The seductive aroma of ripe grapes hanging on vines entices him, and immediately he becomes enamored by their luscious allure. And so begins his ambitious quest up treacherous branches arching past rough bark—an obstacle course stood between him and the desired plump fruit.

However, no matter how many attempts made or schemes devised, our protagonist finds himself slipping further away from his original goal—tasting those tantalizing grapes. Each failure exacerbates his frustration until eventually, he issues an indignant proclamation: "You can keep your precious grapes! They're probably sour anyway."

This cunning twist transforms an apparent defeat into an exercise in self-assurance for our devious fox—a rationalization which mollifies the cognitive dissonance created by circumstance.

Aesop's age-old tale highlights not only man's propensity to face conflicting beliefs head-on but also reveals our underhanded aptitude for conjuring alternate narratives that often mask ulterior motives. We react defensively when confronted with evidence that challenges our cherished ideals because admitting error strikes at the heart of our fragile egos.

As we venture forward from fables to grim realities, we encounter a chilling episode in history that showcases the tragic consequences when cognitive dissonance escalates to unimaginable levels—The Jonestown Massacre.

In 1978, over 900 men, women, and children tragically lost their lives in a mass murder-suicide orchestrated by the cult leader Jim Jones at his remote settlement named Jonestown in Guyana. As Jones led his followers further down a twisted path, his stringent demands and growing paranoia created an unbearable tension between their initial hope for a utopian society and the brutal reality they faced.

These devoted disciples had given up everything—their money, careers, friends—in pursuit of Jones's vision of community and enlightenment. Their effort to reconcile these conflicting ideas forced them to rationalize away mounting evidence that contradicted the benevolent and egalitarian persona Jones projected.

Cognitive dissonance compelled many followers to stay even as life at Jonestown became increasingly dystopian. Fearful dissenters were met with violent threats; those who managed to escape left behind traumatized allies who told themselves tales of loyalty being tested or of faithless deserters weak-willed or malicious.

This particularly dark chapter evinces how powerful cognitive dissonance can be when intensified by isolation from outside perspectives and compounded by relentless indoctrination—all crucial components solidifying one's belief system against any threat posed by dissenting voices. The psychological shackles bore down heavily on Jonestown inhabitants' spirits—an ever-present reminder that choosing anything beyond blind compliance would unyoke their conviction that they had found salvation amid chaos—until it was too late.

Understanding this tragic event through the lens of cognitive dissonance helps us look beyond simplistic assumptions that may dismiss these individuals as weak-minded or gullible; instead revealing a complex web of desires, emotional needs, and cognitive struggles that binds us all as human beings. A vulnerable mind is an easy prey for cunning masters of manipulation who artfully exploit cognitive dissonance to make people doubt the truth in front of their eyes; hence it is crucial that we recognize its unsettling potential and seek ways to mitigate our susceptibility to its deadly charms.

16

The trouble with chance

Our relationship with probability is fraught with misunderstandings and incorrect intuitions, which often lead to perplexing errors in reasoning even among the brightest of minds. Let us now embark on an exploration of some common misconceptions that ensnare our perception of probability and random events.

Our innate need to find patterns combined with the complexity of probability creates the perfect storm for misleading interpretations, such as the Monty Hall Problem.

The renowned game show "Let's Make a Deal" unwittingly spawned one of the most fascinating enigmas in probability—the Monty Hall Problem, named after its eponymous host. This paradox demonstrates how confounding probabilities can become tangled amidst our intuitive judgments—a captivating reminder to reassess our decision-making processes.

Picture yourself as a contestant on the show, presented with three doors concealing two goats and a car—your coveted prize glinting behind only one of these barriers. Initially, you choose a door at whim (let's say Door #1). Host Monty Hall then reveals a goat behind another unchosen door (Door

91

#3, for example), now leaving two remaining doors. He asks you whether you would like to stick with your original choice or switch to Door #2. What should be your strategy?

Contrary to one's initial instinct that both options offer equal likelihoods of success, mathematics in fact counsels otherwise: You stand twice as likely—two-thirds probability, indeed—to win the car if you switch your choice rather than remain loyal to your prime selection.

Laying bare the skeleton beneath this counterintuitive vestige unravels a Gordian knot: When you first picked Door #1, there was a one-third chance it led to victory while an aggregate two-thirds chance crowned either Door #2 or Door #3 triumphant. Monty Hall peeled back a veil from this amalgamated prospect by unveiling a goat behind Door #3; consequently, that previously stealthy two-thirds probability hastened entirely into Door #2.

Let's pause for a moment and revisit this idea, as it may not seem intuitive at first glance. We want to make sure it's crystal clear.

When you first selected a door (Door #1), there was indeed a 1 in 3 chance that it hid the car and a combined 2 in 3 chance that either Door #2 or Door #3 did. Importantly, this initial choice has not changed—the probability associated with your initial selection remains anchored at one-third.

Now comes Monty Hall's intervention; he reveals a goat behind one of the unchosen doors—let's say Door #3. Crucially, Monty does not make this revelation randomly but does so deliberately because he knows which door conceals the car. This action unveils new information about the remaining unchosen door (Door #2) without altering your original door's chances.

Since we know that initially there was a 2 in 3 chance of winning by selecting Door #2 or Door #3 together—and now that we are certain there is no car behind Door #3—all that probability collapses upon Door #2. Thus, shifting to this door will raise your chances of winning from one-third to two-thirds or make it twice as likely compared to sticking with your original choice.

While the Monty Hall Problem exposes the intricacies of grasping probability in specific scenarios, the Gambler's Fallacy exposes a psychological vulnerability we all share when trying to intuit probabilities in broader contexts. Consequently, pondering its roots enriches our exploration of the seductive pitfalls that ensnare us when venturing into the realm of uncertain outcomes.

To truly grasp the nature of the gambler's fallacy, it is essential to dissect the core belief that underpins this all too common cognitive trap. At the heart of the gambler's fallacy is the mistaken belief that a series of independent events have a cause-and-effect relationship. But what does this mean, and how does it manifest in our everyday lives?

In its simplest form, the gambler's fallacy can be defined as the fallacious belief that past events influence future outcomes, when in fact, the events are fundamentally unrelated. It is the flawed assumption that a certain result is more likely to occur, given a series of contrary results in the previous attempts, despite the reality that each event is completely independent.

To move away from abstract definitions and ground this phenomenon in tangible examples, consider the notion of flipping a coin. We all know that the odds of a coin landing on heads or tails are even. And yet, if one were to flip the coin several times and obtain a streak of five heads, the gambler's fallacy might lead us to predict that the next flip would be more likely to result in tails. The disturbing truth, however, is that the next flip remains equally likely to be either heads or tails, regardless of the prior outcomes.

The illustrious Monte Carlo Casino in Monaco has long been a playground for the world's rich and famous. Opulent and grand, it serves as a stage upon which dreams are chased and fortunes are won or, more often than not, lost. It is here at this pinnacle of casino opulence that we find an extraordinary tale that illustrates the puzzling grip of the gambler's fallacy.

On a fateful summer night in 1913, a seemingly ordinary game of roulette began. Spectators gathered around the wheel, eagerly placing their bets as the croupier - the overseer of the game - set the wheel in motion. Little did they know that they were about to witness history.

As the first few spins turned up red, intrigue and curiosity filled the air. With each successive red outcome, the amazement of the onlookers grew. Remarkably, the streak continued unabated, with a staggering 26 red outcomes in a row. The odds of such a sequence occurring were so vanishingly small that it seemed as if the fates themselves had conspired to baffle those present.

This stunning run of red squares brought the workings of the gambler's fallacy into full view. Believing that the next spin simply had to result in the black outcome, many bettors placed extravagant sums of money on black. The absurdity of their logic was lost amidst the mesmerizing backdrop of the win-or-lose drama that unfolded before them. And yet, the wheel continued to betray their hopes, and red reigned supreme.

As we know now, the streak was merely a product of chance. The color on each spin was as unpredictable and independent as the flip of a coin. But those who fell prey to the gambler's fallacy were unable to accept this truth - their minds succumbing to the allure of causality and patterns.

The gambler's fallacy emerges from a complex web of psychological factors. Unraveling this web allows us to better appreciate and confront our susceptibility to falling into this beguiling trap.

A cornerstone of the gambler's fallacy is our natural inclination to recognize patterns. On the savannahs of our ancestral past, spotting recurring patterns endowed us with significant survival advantages. Interpreting patterns in the tracks left by prey, the onset of seasonal changes, and the behavior of other tribe members empowered us to adapt, anticipate, and ultimately survive. This pattern recognition process became so deeply ingrained in the human experience that we began to seek patterns even in random events, just as we do with the flip of a coin or the spin of a roulette wheel.

It is essential to understand that our minds gravitate towards causality – the belief that behind each event lies a tangible cause. Causation helps us make sense of the world and endows us with a sense of control. Consequently, when we mistakenly believe in a causal link between independent events, the gambler's fallacy is not far behind. This desire for causality, coupled with our aforementioned love for patterns, fuels our fallacious thinking, tempting us into believing that the outcomes of unrelated events can influence one another.

Another contributing factor is our struggle with randomness. Human minds grapple with the concept of random phenomena, preferring, instead, to cling to the idea of order and structure. The gambler's fallacy tempts us by offering a soothing illusion of predictability in a world governed, in part, by the caprices of chance. It caters to our longing for control in a universe indifferent to our desires.

Lastly, as social creatures, we are vulnerable to the lure of anecdotal evidence. Hearing a friend's account of a winning formula at a casino or a relative's streak of good (or bad) luck may seduce us into adopting the gambler's fallacy. Overwhelmed by the richness of personal stories, we tend to overlook the statistical probabilities that should inform our decisions. Instead, we're swayed by the compelling narratives that resonate more profoundly with our emotions and imagination.

The Monte Carlo Casino's tale is a testament to the pervasiveness of the gambler's fallacy, irrespective of one's education, social standing, or, indeed, familiarity with the games at hand. This phenomenon compels us to question the very underpinnings of our decision-making processes and appreciate the necessity for intellectual humility - the recognition that even the seemingly rational minds among us are not immune to the siren call of flawed logic.

17

The belief in a fair and ordered universe

I t would be far too facile to consider the human tendency to search for patterns and succumb to cognitive biases as a mere curiosity without delving deeper into the psychological architecture that allows these errors of reasoning to flourish. Another bias that humans fall prey to, the just-world hypothesis is one that sheds light on our profound desire to make sense of the world from a moral standpoint.

The just-world hypothesis, in its essence, refers to the belief that the world is fundamentally fair and that actions and consequences are intrinsically interlinked. Under this assumption, one's experiences are drawn from a cosmic balance of moral justice, wherein reward accompanies virtue and misfortune befalls those who err.

At a glance, the allure of such a hypothesis is undeniable. Envisioning a just world provides a level of emotional comfort, instilling us with a sense of control and predictability. As already covered, our cognitive machinery is hardwired to find patterns, explanations, and causality within the chaos of existence. It is in this landscape that the just-world hypothesis takes root, providing a framework for meaning and order, even when the world operates with apparent randomness or indifference.

At the heart of this hypothesis lies the principle of moral reasoning and its most fundamental iteration, the concept of cause and effect. The human mind naturally ascribes rewards and punishments to fit the moral narrative we have concocted in our search for meaning. Our experiences and observations seem to mandatorily undergo this filter, as the mind persistently seeks out moral equilibrium in the landscape of life. The just-world hypothesis, similar to the gambler's fallacy, elucidates our predisposition to find causality and pattern where perhaps randomness holds the reigns.

Despite its simplicity, it is a powerful force that shapes our perception of the world. While seemingly innocuous, the just-world hypothesis has important implications for social and interpersonal relationships, as will be explored in later sections.

To bring this concept to life, let us consider the age-old adage: "What goes around comes around." We rely on this phrase to assert that those who engage in good deeds will eventually see the return of their benevolence in some form or another. Simultaneously, we are also implying that individuals who act maliciously or selfishly will, in due course, receive the negative consequences that they deserve. This saying, woven into the fabric of our cultural lexicon, exemplifies the just-world hypothesis' underlying assumptions.

It is important to recognize that the just-world hypothesis is not necessarily an unfounded belief system. In many instances, people's behavior indeed triggers corresponding consequences, particularly in structured societies with well-defined laws and norms. For example, when someone stays late at work, diligently completing a project, they may receive praise, a promotion, or a raise—a clear illustration of good behavior yielding a positive result. On the other hand, a reckless driver who frequently exceeds the speed limit may face fines, license suspension, or even an accident—an evidently negative outcome stemming from their behavior.

However, the just-world hypothesis leads to difficulties when facing situations where the relationship between behavior and consequence is not so evident or, in some cases, where it may be absent altogether. If we stay entrenched within the belief in a just world, we might wrestle with cognitive dissonance when attempting to make sense of ambiguous and complex realities. In some situations, the just-world hypothesis pushes us to oversimplify and misinterpret experiences and events, leading to an illusory sense of understanding.

Attaching a sense of fairness to the world can bring about feelings of reassurance and emotional stability. Imagine the anxiety if we viewed life as a roulette table, where events were governed not by well-defined mechanisms, but by random, uncontrollable forces. By assuming that there exists a moral order underpinning the events that we encounter, we can maintain our sanity and find solace in the notion that our decisions have consequences in a manner that is sensible and comprehensible.

This innate inclination towards a just and orderly world can be immensely beneficial in terms of individual self-motivation, ambition, and emotional stability. Concurrently, however, it can interfere with a clear-sighted understanding of the world around us, leading us to ignore or overlook circumstances where justice and fairness may not be at work. A flexible, nuanced understanding of the world demands the realization that life's outcomes do not always adhere to the simplistic framework of actions followed by proportionate consequences.

The beloved children's story "The Little Engine That Could" has been inspiring children and adults alike for generations. The central character, a small and somewhat inefficient engine, perseveres against all odds and manages to surmount a seemingly insurmountable obstacle through sheer determination and single-minded, unwavering effort. This heartwarming tale not only propounds the value of persistence and self-belief but also exemplifies the just-world mindset in action: everything works out in the end for those who try hard enough.

Though this narrative is undeniably uplifting and morally instructive, it subtly encourages the idea that success is solely the result of hard work and internal determination. Cinderella stories such as this one are certainly appealing - who hasn't dreamt of surmounting every challenge in their way with the power of self-belief and grit? Unfortunately, life's harsh realities often suggest that the world does not always reward resilience and commitment with commensurate success.

Parables like "The Little Engine That Could" unwittingly nurture the just-world hypothesis, instilling in us an often-unrealistic belief that individuals in unfortunate situations have merely fallen victim to their own deficiencies. The danger of this worldview lies in its capacity to breed complacency and indifference to the systemic barriers that some people face daily. The story, while inspiring, can inadvertently lead us to place the burden of failure or success squarely on the individual, with little consideration given to the contextual forces at work.

A more troubling and consequential example that illustrates the power of the just-world hypothesis can be found in the system of apartheid that plagued South Africa for nearly five decades. This brutal legal regime was built on the cornerstone of racial segregation and the systematic deprivation of the country's non-white majority. Apartheid was maintained through a series of draconian laws designed to restrict every aspect of black South Africans' lives, from where they lived to how they worked—even who they could love.

For such a perverse and exclusionary system to persist, those at the top needed to justify their policies and convince a significant portion of the population that these policies were fair. This is where the just-world hypothesis came into play. Proponents of apartheid relied heavily on a narrative of the deserving and the undeserving, a clash between the hard-working white minority who had built the nation and the supposedly lesser non-white majority who sought to reap the rewards without earning them.

Apartheid was sold to many South Africans as a necessary, moral, and even divine system that sought to maintain order and protect the fruits of hard work and calculation. The just-world hypothesis was crucial to maintaining this illusion. By invoking the idea that people get what they deserve, supporters of apartheid were able to justify terrible suffering inflicted upon black South Africans as both necessary and, in some twisted way, deserved.

The iniquitous legacy of apartheid lends credence to the potential dangers of the just-world hypothesis. What appears to be a simple belief in the inherent fairness of the world, when taken to an extreme, can justify even the most abhorrent cruelties and exclusions.

18

When every victory comes with a cost

At the heart of several cognitive biases and fallacies, an underlying mindset often emerges: zero-sum thinking. This concept is steeped in the belief that any given situation has a fixed amount of resources, rewards, or success, and the only way to acquire these is by competing and outperforming others. In essence, zero-sum thinking implies that one person's gain is invariably another's loss; this belief engenders competition, accumulation, and exclusionary tactics.

To explain this concept with a simple, everyday example, imagine a scenario where two siblings are each given a cookie by their mother. The young siblings view these cookies as valuable commodities and cannot imagine a world where other treats might abound. They begin to see their treats as a fixed resource, and before long, they are absorbed in a frenzied competition to acquire each other's cookies. Rather than enjoying their snacks, the siblings are now consumed by rivalry, believing that having both cookies is the ultimate display of victory. Although the mother could provide more cookies or suggest that they share with each other, the siblings remain imprisoned in their zero-sum mentality, unable to imagine any alternative to their bitter contest.

It's important to clarify that zero-sum thinking is not purely irrational. Situations may indeed arise where resources are genuinely limited, and competition is a logical approach. However, the issue with zero-sum thinking lies in applying this perspective too widely, extending it to scenarios where cooperation, mutual benefit, and even abundance might be readily attainable. In these instances, this mindset evolves from a rational response to a genuine scarcity into an irrational embrace of an unnecessarily limited worldview.

In essence, zero-sum thinking fosters a belief in a fixed-pie mindset—that the world we inhabit is confined by finite resources, and our task is to secure our share, even at others' expense. This worldview can narrow our understanding of complex socio-economic systems, which are often marked by trade-offs, interdependencies, and the potential for mutual gain. By clinging to the assumption that life is an inherently competitive struggle, zero-sum thinking can drive antagonistic attitudes towards others, stifle innovative solutions to shared problems, and hinder the pursuit of common goals.

In order to better understand the grip that zero-sum thinking holds on our minds, we must delve into the psychological origins of this mindset and how it develops over time. Interestingly, zero-sum thinking can be traced back to some of our most primal instincts and the evolutionary pressures that have shaped human behavior.

At the core of zero-sum thinking lies our instinct for self-preservation. In the distant past, our ancestors were confronted with numerous threats to their survival, including competition for limited resources such as food, water, and shelter. In those circumstances, securing essential resources often meant thwarting rivals, thus cultivating the notion that others' losses directly translated to personal gains. From this perspective, zero-sum thinking can be seen as a byproduct of evolution—a mental strategy that once improved our odds of survival but now lingers in our modern world even when it is no longer warranted.

However, zero-sum thinking is not only rooted in evolutionary pressures. It also burgeons from the cognitive shortcuts our minds frequently employ: heuristics. These mental rules of thumb enable us to navigate complex environments and make decisions quickly. Unfortunately, while heuristics can be incredibly useful in some situations, they can also bias our judgments and steer us toward zero-sum thinking. For instance, the tendency to generalize from a few instances based on limited information can contribute to the belief that competition is inevitable in every circumstance.

Social conditioning and cultural practices, too, play a significant role in cultivating zero-sum thinking. From a young age, we are exposed to messages that normalize competition and rivalry as essential aspects of life. In sports, politics, and academic achievements, zero-sum logic is almost implicitly broadcasted: there can only be one winner, and others must inevitably lose. This paradigm permeates our social fabric, planting the seeds of zero-sum thinking in impressionable minds and reinforcing the mental model throughout our lives.

It is also worth noting the role of personality in determining our susceptibility to zero-sum thinking. Psychologists have found that individuals with high levels of narcissism or paranoia are more likely to subscribe to a zero-sum worldview. These personality traits foster a preoccupation with social comparisons, threats, and domination, all of which can contribute to the belief that life is an unending battle for scarce resources.

To further illuminate the limits of zero-sum thinking, let's venture into the realm of game theory and explore a classic scenario known as the prisoner's dilemma. This thought experiment underscores how a seemingly rational zero-sum approach can trap us in suboptimal outcomes, while the pursuit of cooperation can unlock mutual benefits.

Imagine two accomplices arrested for a crime and held in separate cells, unable to communicate. The prosecutor presents each of them with a stark choice: either betray their partner and testify against them in exchange for a lighter sentence or remain silent and hope their partner does the same. If both prisoners betray each other, they will each receive a moderately severe sentence. If one betrays but the other remains silent, the betrayer walks free while the loyal partner receives the most severe sentence. However, if both prisoners stay silent, they will receive the lightest punishment.

In this scenario, a zero-sum mindset would lead each prisoner to assume that betraying their partner is the safest course of action. After all, under the assumption that only one's gain must come at the other's expense, self-interest seems to dictate betrayal to secure at least a moderately severe sentence rather than risk the harshest punishment. And yet, both prisoners ultimately fare better if they both remain silent and choose the path of cooperation over betrayal.

What the prisoner's dilemma so elegantly reveals is the fallacy that can arise when we cling to zero-sum thinking in situations where mutual gains are possible. Despite our instincts to safeguard ourselves by outmatching our rivals, we inadvertently undermine our collective best interests. If the prisoners could step outside the constraints of zero-sum thinking, they would recognize that trust and cooperation would lead to a more desirable outcome for both.

Although the prisoner's dilemma is admittedly artificial, it serves as an instructive metaphor for various real-world situations in which zero-sum thinking stifles our ability to envision cooperative solutions. By disregarding the possibility of mutual gains, zero-sum thinking compels us to perpetuate needless conflict and antagonism.

To better grasp the real-world implications of zero-sum thinking, let us examine its role in two arenas where it frequently arises: economic and political competition. Considering the belief that one's success necessitates another's failure, it is no surprise that these contentious spheres often fall prey to zero-sum influences.

In economic competition, the pursuit of finite resources can drive a perception that one party's gain equates to another's loss. For instance, businesses struggling for market share or nations vying for scarce minerals might be lured into the trap of zero-sum thinking. This mindset can manifest as ruthless tactics, such as aggressively undercutting prices, attempting hostile takeovers, or waging price wars, as each player seeks to outperform its rivals. However, this zero-sum tunnel vision can obscure the potential for collaborative strategies that could unlock benefits for all parties involved.

A prime example lies in the rise of collaborative consumption and the sharing economy, which present a different avenue for addressing resource scarcity. Instead of being entrenched in ruthless competition, businesses and individuals can share underutilized resources to create more value for everyone, transforming a potentially zero-sum scenario into one with mutual benefits. Platforms like Airbnb and Uber exemplify this breakthrough, enabling individuals to share their idle homes and vehicles to create additional income while offering services to a broader segment of the population.

Likewise, zero-sum thinking can infiltrate the political sphere, where factions vie for control and influence, often assuming that any progress or victory for their adversaries equates to a loss for themselves. This divisive mindset can rigidify party lines and hinder constructive dialogue, as each camp seeks to "win" rather than collaborate, unwittingly stifling efforts to address the multidimensional issues societies face.

Despite these tendencies, there exist striking examples of nations overcoming the zero-sum mindset on the political stage, leading to groundbreaking advances that benefit multiple parties at once. The European Union, born from the ashes of World War II, exemplifies a triumph of collaborative thinking, as historically warring nations joined forces to achieve peace and prosperity by pooling their resources and fostering economic interdependence. Recognizing that rivalry and conflict produce only mutual losses, these nations have embraced a paradigm of cooperation that yields more substantial gains for all involved.

19

Unraveling the Myth of Autonomy

It's crucial to consider the possibility that our steadfast belief in our own autonomy might, in fact, be our most profound and pervasive misconception. This potential misapprehension trumps even the most notorious cognitive biases, skewing our perspectives and distorting our grasp on reality as we navigate our lives. As the inquisitive thinkers we consider ourselves to be, it's essential to explore in depth how the apparent illusion of free will may cloud our judgment and, in doing so, reveal the stark disconnect between our perception and the truth that lies beneath the surface.

Throughout history, philosophers have grappled with the concept of free will, debating whether our choices are genuinely ours to make or simply a product of deterministic forces beyond our control. At the core of the free will debate is the question of human autonomy - the extent to which we are capable of dictating our own paths and the degree of responsibility we hold for the outcomes that arise from our actions.

The implications of free will extend far beyond the realm of philosophy, permeating our psychological, moral, and societal perceptions of individual accountability. If we believe our decisions are indeed the product of our volition, we are more inclined to hold ourselves and others responsible for their actions, attributing consequences to acts of free choice and using concepts such as blame, praise, reward, and punishment as tools to enforce the conduct we collectively deem acceptable.

In supporting our belief in free will, we garner a heightened sense of personal control and potential - a foundation from which we construct our individual narratives and aspirations. This belief grants us the conviction that we possess agency and that our life's trajectory is shaped by the sum of our choices and efforts.

However, as alluring as this freedom may seem, recent advances in neuro-science, psychology, and sociology call into question the extent to which our belief in free will aligns with reality. As we delve deeper into the true nature of our autonomy, we must ask ourselves: Are the choices we make truly our own, or are they merely the product of a complex tapestry of influences that exist beyond our conscious awareness? By exploring this contentious terrain, we hope to foster intellectual humility and enhance our understanding of the power and limits inherent in our perceived autonomy.

Our perception of free will is an intricate mosaic of influences, dictated in part by psychological mechanisms and societal norms that serve to maintain the delicate balance of personal autonomy and collective control.

First, let us examine the role of psychology in shaping our beliefs about free will. Our cognitive architecture is finely tuned to prioritize intentions, desires, and beliefs when accounting for our actions and planning our behaviors. This propensity for agentic thinking fosters the emergence of a self-narrative wherein we are the autonomous protagonists charting our unique journey through life. Moreover, our inclination to discern patterns and causality in the world around us prompts us to assign authorship and responsibility for the outcomes we observe, ourselves being at the epicenter of such attributions.

Crucially, our belief in free will is not only a product of cognitive mechanisms, but it is also intimately intertwined with our emotions and our sense of self-worth. Research has shown that when our actions result in negative consequences, we are more inclined to attribute them to external forces to alleviate the sting of guilt and preserve our self-esteem. Conversely, positive outcomes augment our belief in our agency, cementing our confidence in our capacity to choose and act freely.

The reach of societal forces in sculpting our understanding of free will extends far and wide. Educational systems, religious institutions, and cultural traditions all share a common thread of promoting the value of personal choice and individual responsibility. For the smooth functioning of societies, it is imperative that citizens understand their decisions as grounded in autonomy so that accountability and a moral compass can be upheld.

The influence of renowned historical figures and philosophical ideologies on our perspective of free will cannot be overstated. The convergence of existentialist thought, championed by the likes of Jean-Paul Sartre and Friedrich Nietzsche, and Enlightenment ideals of self-determination, championed by John Locke and Immanuel Kant, has nurtured a cultural climate wherein the importance of autonomy and free choice remain largely unquestionable. We are raised to view our lives as a series of branching paths, each turning point determined by our unfettered will, each decision sowing the seeds of our future accomplishments or failures.

In examining our free will as deliberate agents, it would be remiss to separate the mind from the complex workings of the brain. John-Dylan Haynes, a renowned neuroscientist, has performed groundbreaking experiments that provide us with a fascinating window into the neural basis of decision-making. Haynes' work, at the intersection of philosophy and neuroscience, calls into question some of our most deeply held assumptions about free will and personal autonomy.

At the core of Haynes' experiments lies a deceptively simple yet elegant design. Participants are asked to lay in a functional magnetic resonance imaging (fMRI) scanner while being presented with a sequence of randomized letters on a screen. They are instructed to freely decide at any moment to press one of two buttons either with their left or right hand. Upon making the decision, the subjects are to note the letter that was displayed at the time of their choice. While the participants believe they are exerting free will in deciding when and with which hand to press the button, Haynes and his team are observing brain activity in real-time to make startling revelations.

In a landmark study, Haynes and his colleagues discovered that certain patterns of brain activity could predict the timing and hand choice of the button press up to ten seconds before the participant consciously made the decision. Remarkably, the participants remained wholly unaware of the neural processes underpinning their choices, believing their actions to be products of conscious, voluntary control.

The implications of Haynes' experiments are vast. If decisions are discernable in neural activity even before they enter our conscious awareness, how can it be claimed that these choices are made with genuine free will? Can we genuinely reconcile our deeply ingrained beliefs about personal freedom and our capacity to make autonomous choices with the reality of our brains as biological machines, governed by a complex interplay of unseen forces?

Consider the following thought experiment, designed to help you reflect on the nature of your choices and the role of free will in your decision-making process:

Imagine you're standing in front of two doors, each door adorned with either a vibrant red or a calm blue hue. You're tasked with deciding which door you will walk through, with no indication of what may lie behind them. As you contemplate your choice, pause for a moment to consider the multitude of factors at work in this seemingly simple decision.

What factors are guiding your choice? Do you prefer the color red or blue? Is it a result of personal experiences or cultural associations with each color? Can you locate your choice's origin within your thought processes, or are the reasons lying in a realm hidden beneath conscious awareness?

Take a moment to reflect on the neural activity that accompanies your thought process. Recall Haynes' findings that such activity can predict decisions long before they surface in our conscious minds. Now, consider whether your decision is rooted in free will or is a product of your brain's intricate workings. Is it possible that the factors influencing your choice extend beyond your awareness, into a complex network of hidden influences?

As we delve further into the realms of our decision-making processes, we inevitably come face to face with the vast and enigmatic sea of the subconscious. The notion that we are mostly unaware of the innumerable factors influencing our everyday choices can be an unsettling realization, one that inevitably looms over our deeply held beliefs in personal autonomy and free will. This invisible hand of the subconscious operates in the background of our lives, governing the choices we make with astonishing precision.

Let us consider the psychological concept of priming. In a now-classic study by John Bargh and his colleagues at New York University, participants in the experiment were unobtrusively primed with words relating to the elderly – such as "Florida," "bingo," and "wrinkles" - while engaged in a seemingly unrelated task. Upon completing the task, the participants walked down a hallway, unknowingly becoming the subject of the real experiment: their walking speed had been significantly reduced, mimicking the slow gait of the elderly. The subtlety with which unconscious priming shaped their behavior revealed the astonishing power of the subconscious mind over our conscious actions.

In another example, individuals' generosity can be influenced by simple environmental factors. Studies have demonstrated that participants placed in a room infused with the scent of freshly baked bread, often associated with warmth and comfort, display more charitable behavior and are more willing to help others compared to those in unscented rooms. This seemingly minor change in the environment has far-reaching effects on our decision-making processes that operate beneath the veil of conscious thought.

The undeniable role played by the subconscious mind in our choices raises profound questions about the nature of free will. To what extent are we truly masters of our destiny? Are we mere puppets, with our subconscious mind pulling invisible strings that govern our actions? Can we truly lay claim to our achievements or bear the burden of our mistakes if subconscious influences beyond our control direct our decisions?

As our understanding of the role of the subconscious and the myriad factors influencing our decisions expands, the repercussions of questioning free will on human behavior and ethics lead us to a pivotal crossroad. To confront the ethical implications of these discoveries, we must be willing to immerse ourselves in a world of inquiry where conventional wisdom is left at the doorstep, and we allow our most cherished beliefs to be scrutinized in the light of new evidence.

In the absence of complete autonomy, the concept of personal accountability may appear to be tenuous. If our choices are, in fact, orchestrated by a symphony of external factors and subconscious influences, can we truly be held accountable for our actions? This question gives rise to concerns about the implications of questioning free will on moral responsibility. Can our notions of right and wrong, good and evil stand on firm ground if our actions are rigged from the outset?

The issue of retribution faces similar challenges in the wake of these revelations. If the assumption of free will is dismantled, can we justly penalize individuals for their misconduct? Can we hold them responsible for their actions if those actions were determined by forces beyond their control? Confronting the relationship between free will, retribution, and justice requires a fundamental reassessment of the principles upon which our legal and penal systems are built.

As daunting as these questions may seem, we must not evade the responsibility of confronting them head-on. Questioning the assumption of free will calls for a more nuanced and sophisticated understanding of human behavior and ethics. Embracing this reality can bring about a greater sense of intellectual humility, as we recognize the limitations of our will and discern the impact of the countless variables that forge our decisions.

In the face of these challenges, we might look to the concept of compatibilism as a means to navigate the murky waters of free will and determinism in our ethical frameworks. Compatibilism puts forth the notion that free will can coexist with determinism - that individuals can be considered free agents while recognizing that their choices are, to some degree, influenced by external and subconscious factors. This perspective allows us to hold individuals morally responsible without undermining the importance of these forces that shape our decision-making processes.

By fostering intellectual humility and acknowledging the pivotal role that hidden influences play in our lives, we can strive to mitigate the impact of subconscious biases and environmental factors on our decision-making. With intention, awareness, and practice, we can cultivate a heightened sense of mindfulness and develop a more profound respect for the complexity of the human experience.

In this pursuit, we must embrace critical thinking and self-reflection, as it is through these practices that we can strive to disentangle ourselves from the web of biases, fallacies, and societal pressures that obscure our true intentions. By fostering a renewed sense of intellectual humility, we might be better equipped to reevaluate the ethical implications of our decisions and craft a more enlightened and compassionate understanding of responsibility, morality, and retribution.

As we wrestle with the idea that the invisible hand of the subconscious shapes our decisions, we are also compelled to reexamine our deeply held convictions about personal accountability, moral responsibility, and retribution. How do we reconcile this newfound understanding of the human mind with the centuries-old systems of ethics, laws, and morality upon which our societies are built?

Take the concept of personal accountability, for example. While we generally view ourselves as responsible agents of our choices and actions, the acknowledgment that our decision-making process is shaped by subconscious priming and unseen environmental factors muddles the waters of accountability. How can we claim authorship over our decisions if external forces far beyond our control are quietly orchestrating our actions? This question challenges us to revisit our judgments of right and wrong, the very foundations upon which our social contracts rest.

Plunging deeper into this thought, we must confront the implications of our subconscious influences on moral responsibility. Indeed, the moral fabric of society necessitates the attribution of responsibility to the individuals making choices - whether they be ethical or unethical. The concept of moral responsibility, however, becomes entangled with the nuanced workings of the subconscious mind, subsequently casting a shadow over our established moral tenets. Are we genuinely guilty of immoral acts if they are, in part, a product of subconscious forces beyond our conscious recognition? This query beckons us towards a profound reevaluation of what it means to be morally responsible, pushing us to the boundaries of traditional ethical understanding.

Ultimately, delving into the heart of justice, we grapple with the notion of retribution. Punishment, as a fundamental component of virtually all human societies, stems from our conviction that people must bear the consequences of their wrongdoings. Here, again, the omnipresent role of the subconscious raises undeniably challenging dilemmas. If the invisible masters of our subconscious significantly influence our decisions, to what extent can we justify punishing individuals for their actions? Should retribution still be meted out in a world where personal autonomy is persistently cast in doubt?

This staggering uncertainty surrounding the nature of our free will puts us in an unsettling conundrum. By stripping away the veneer of autonomy, we are forced to confront a myriad of uncertainties that challenge the foundations of our beliefs, values, and judgments. Grappling with these uncertainties invites us to embrace intellectual humility at its core; that is to say, admitting that "I don't know" might just be a better starting point in our quest for truth and self-understanding.

20

When letting go is the smarter choice

As we dissect the intricacies of the sunk cost fallacy, it is essential first to establish a firm understanding of this pervasive cognitive misjudgment. Drawing its roots from decision theory and behavioral economics, the sunk cost fallacy describes the tendency of individuals to persist with a failing or detrimental course of action, simply because they have already invested significant time, money, or effort into it. In essence, the fallacy materializes when we erroneously factor unrecoverable, "sunk" costs into our decision-making processes, leading us down a murky path of emotional entanglements and irrational choices.

At the core of this fallacy lies the profoundly human aversion to loss. As social beings with a predisposition towards stability and low-risk endeavors, we often refuse to abandon a sinking ship, desperately clinging to the misplaced belief that further investments will somehow redeem the already sunk costs. As a result, we become embroiled in a quagmire of escalating commitment, rooted more in our psychological attachment to past decisions than in their present viability.

To appreciate the subtle but pervasive influence of the sunk cost fallacy on our lives, we must delve into its mechanics, beginning with a clear understanding of opportunity costs. Sometimes overlooked in the decision-making process, opportunity costs refer to the potential benefits that we forgo when choosing one course of action over another. By becoming entangled in the sunk cost fallacy, we inflate the value of our failing commitments and, in doing so, disregard the unexplored advantages that alternative paths may offer. Tragically, it is this very blindness to opportunity costs that often perpetuates a spiraling cycle of detrimental investments, like gambling addicts throwing good money after bad.

It is also important to recognize that the sunk cost fallacy does not discriminate between investment types. Emotional investments, such as time and effort, can be just as influential in driving the fallacy as concrete resources like money. Consequently, we face the sunk cost fallacy's treacherous grip in various domains of our lives: from pouring resources into poor business choices, to persisting in toxic relationships in the hope of salvaging a perceived worth.

As we move towards untangling the web of the sunk cost fallacy, we are confronted with the undeniable influences of loss aversion. A fundamental aspect of human psychology, loss aversion postulates that we are intrinsically more sensitive to the prospect of losses than we are to gains, experiencing the sting of potential loss more acutely than the allure of potential reward. It is within the nuances of this underlying psychological principle that the roots of the sunk cost fallacy become entwined, forging a seemingly inescapable nexus between these two cognitive vulnerabilities.

Loss aversion propels us into the arms of the sunk cost fallacy by fostering a distorted view of the value proposition at play. Guided by the prism of loss aversion, we erroneously weigh the pain of "losing" our initial investment more heavily than the potential benefits of cutting our losses and pursuing alternative routes. This skewed perception of value leads to a domino effect, wherein we compound our losses by refusing to let go of a fruitless endeavor, thus perpetuating the sunk cost fallacy.

A closer examination reveals that the interaction between loss aversion and the sunk cost fallacy can manifest in myriad ways. To illustrate, imagine a scenario in which one endures the discomfort of a toxic work environment. Here, our inherent loss aversion and an almost visceral reluctance to acknowledge wasted time and effort perniciously work in tandem, culminating in a disquieting decision to stay. Driven by the irrational belief that leaving would render past investments futile, the individual sacrifices future fulfillment for the preservation of a sinking status quo.

Another salient example appears in the arena of failed marriages or romantic relationships where considerable emotional and financial investments have been made. It is not uncommon for individuals to remain entrenched in these caustic emotional landscapes, despite ample evidence that continuing down that path will only heighten the misery. Here too, loss aversion breeds a misplaced attachment to the idea that breaking away would automatically render the years and sacrifices as "wasted," thus compelling the afflicted individual to continue in a desperate but futile effort to evade emotional bankruptcy.

In order to deepen our understanding of the sunk cost fallacy, we must venture into the realm of real-life applications that elucidate how even the brightest and most capable minds can fall prey to its seductive grasp. Perhaps no better example exists than the Concorde aircraft project – a beautifully ambitious and technologically advanced endeavor plagued by mismanagement, wilful blindness, and ultimately, an unwavering attachment to sunk costs.

The 1960s witnessed a world entranced by the promise of supersonic commercial air travel, with the collaboration between the British Aircraft Corporation and France's Aérospatiale culminating in a united commitment to turning this dream into reality. The Concorde, as it came to be known, was a symbol of innovation, prestige, and an air of aristocracy – a winged embodiment of a new era in transportation set to propel the industry into the stratosphere, both literally and figuratively.

Yet beneath the surface of the Concorde's shimmering facade lay a host of challenges and drawbacks that cast a dark and ominous shadow on the project. Skyrocketing costs, deafening sonic booms, and a limited market converged into a tumultuous storm of impediments and shortcomings to which the project's champions were resistant. Despite the increasing doubt surrounding the Concorde's economic viability in light of competition from more efficient and affordable subsonic aircraft, the commitment to the project remained steadfast and immovable.

It was in the throes of this mounting uncertainty that the sunk cost fallacy held sway, blinding the project's proponents to the dire implications of their unwavering resolve. Initial investments, stratospheric expectations, and political pressures acquainted with the diplomatic stage conspired to reinforce a stubborn, steely grip on the Concorde's future. The reluctance to admit failure and the desire to cling to the prestige associated with the superseding jet led to a damaging cycle of escalating commitment and a corresponding resistance to the glaring evidence of the endeavor's doomed prospects.

By the time the Concorde fleet was ultimately retired in 2003, the passionate and lofty ambitions of the 1960s had been replaced by the harsh and unforgiving reality of an economically unsustainable project. The Concorde's discontinuation stemmed from a tragic accident in 2000 that severely waned public confidence and rendered the aircraft's economics irretrievably unviable. The financial and opportunity costs of the failed project served as a sobering reminder of the dangers of persisting with a faltering enterprise, held captive by the enthralling embrace of the sunk cost fallacy.

As we survey the wreckage of the Concorde's storied past, we glean an invaluable lesson in the power that the sunk cost fallacy can wield over even the most sophisticated and prodigious intellects.

In our quest to understand the sunk cost fallacy's influence, we turn from the lofty heights of aviation to the more intimate sphere of personal relationships and everyday decisions. Here, in a quieter but no less profound arena, the sunk cost fallacy manifests its power, dictating our choices and preventing us from acknowledging the truth about the relationships and paths that no longer serve us well.

Under the spell of the sunk cost fallacy, long-term romantic partnerships that have lost their vitality may be sustained purely because of the investments made in time, emotion, and shared experiences. With each day that slides into the annals of the past, the psychological weight of what has been invested grows heavier, prompting couples to ignore the present in favor of a misguided quest to salvage the past. This defiance of the present state of the relationship, fueled by the fallacy, can lead to prolonged unhappiness and the erosion of individual and mutual growth.

Friendships are similarly susceptible to the sunk cost fallacy. Long-standing connections can appear impenetrable, given the treasure trove of shared memories, laughter, and mutual support that feeds into our mental investments. However, as people continue to grow and evolve, the initial compatibility that once provided the foundation for such friendships could recede with the passage of time. Adhering to the sunk cost fallacy may prevent us from reevaluating these relationships, stifling our potential for growth and expansion by clinging to a past that no longer reflects the present.

Familial bonds, too, cannot escape the grasp of the sunk cost fallacy. Parents may invest a substantial amount of their resources, time, and hopes into their children's futures, neglecting to recognize when a change of course might be in the best interests of all parties involved. Similarly, adult children may maintain unhealthy or draining relationships with relatives, feeling an unwarranted obligation rooted in shared history, succumbing to the deceptive allure of the sunk cost fallacy.

Our choices regarding education and careers can also become entwined in the confounding web of sunk costs. Completing a degree or training that no longer aligns with our passions and aspirations can feel obligatory purely because of the investments of time, money, and effort already expended. This humbling recognition can be profoundly difficult to accept, leaving us vulnerable to the trap of the sunk cost fallacy.

The same applies to financial investments, where the sunk cost fallacy can foster an aversion to acknowledging failure. In situations where we have poured significant resources into an asset that has since depreciated, it can be challenging to let go and cut our losses. The sunk cost fallacy in this situation only exacerbates our inherent sense of loss aversion; thus, the act of accepting failure becomes increasingly difficult.

III

Intellectual Humility and the Search for Truth in History

21

Socrates and the wisdom of admitting ignorance

In the dance between intelligence and humility, our minds perform a precarious ballet - ever drawn toward the passionate pursuit of knowledge, yet must remain calculated and poised to avoid the pitfalls of our cognitive shortcomings. It is only by embracing the fundamental duality of our intellect - its astonishing capacity for discovery tempered by an essential acknowledgment of its limitations - that we can truly navigate the challenges that arise in our quest for an ever-elusive truth.

We have borne witness to the complexities of human cognition and the myriad ways in which our faculties can betray our understanding of the world. We have identified, dissected, and scrutinized cognitive biases and fallacies that pervade the human mind, obfuscating reality and leading even the brightest among us into the shadows of ignorance.

Now we shift focus to the redemptive narrative of intellectual humility. In so doing, we shall illuminate the path to enlightenment, drawing on the insights and experiences of those who have dared to tread this treacherous terrain before us and have emerged transformed. Through a historical lens, we shall explore the triumphs and tribulations of these intrepid thinkers in their relentless pursuit of truth, uncovering the essential role of intellectual humility in their revolutionary discoveries.

These venerated figures - ancient and modern, renowned and unsung - embody the spirit of intellectual humility, demonstrating the power of acknowledging the limits of one's knowledge and the immense potential that lies in accepting the unknown. Embracing vulnerable truths, they forged a path through the shadows of uncertainty, illuminating the way forward while simultaneously providing crucial insights into the power of intellectual humility in shaping human history.

Whether traversing the hallowed grounds of ancient Athens, unraveling the mysteries of the cosmos, or defying convention to uncover the threads that hold the fabric of life together, these inspiring thinkers embody the essence of what it means to seek truth with courage and humility.

Our journey begins in the bustling agora of ancient Athens, where a singular figure wanders among the throngs of people, engaging in what would come to be known as the dialectic dance of inquiry, challenging convention and cementing his place as one of the most esteemed philosophers in the annals of human history. As in all things, he both elicits admiration and provokes ire, igniting the spark of curiosity in some while fanning the flames of resentment in others, as he shines a light on the darkest recesses of their minds.

Socrates, enigmatic and transcendent, bestrides the epochs of history, embodying a timeless wisdom that he generously imparts with a disarming humility. His philosophical contributions continue to reverberate across the millennia, gracing the intellectual endeavors of myriad souls who grapple with life's most beguiling questions.

Widely acknowledged as a cornerstone of Western philosophy, Socrates' legacy owes much to the candor with which he approached the lofty ideals of knowledge, truth, and virtue. Rather than clinging to rigid dogma or claiming an infallible understanding, he embraced an intellectual humility that was as astonishingly bold as it was powerful. This self-same humility unleashed a torrent of critical thought and philosophical reckoning that would irrevocably change the course of human history.

So, what was it about Socrates' approach that granted it such profound impact on the intellectual trajectory of mankind? Delve beneath the surface, and one discovers the cornerstone that granted his philosophy enduring resonance: an unwavering commitment to questioning assumptions. This was no frivolous pursuit, but a conscious and deliberate movement away from accepting the dogma and beliefs of society at face value. Such a commitment stemmed from an appreciation of the inherent fallibility of individual minds – including his own – and the resulting imperative to seek collective wisdom through dialogue. This dynamic dance of ideas came to be known as the Socratic method.

Central to the Socratic method is the practice of relentless inquiry. In its essence, it comprises a series of well-structured questions intended to engage the participant's mind, compelling them to thoroughly examine every angle of their initially held beliefs. These questions – though simple in their form – served as powerful catalysts for change: each one designed to expose contradictions, challenge presumptions, and provoke critical thinking. Socrates artfully weaved these verbal tapestries of inquiry with striking nuance, always mindful of the human inclination to defend our views, even when facing the weight of internal contradictions.

One could argue that Socrates breathed new life into the art of dialogue and debate with this question-driven approach. He recognized, quite dramatically, that engaging the intellect of others was essential to creating a fertile ground for the cultivation of wisdom. Instead of fixating on pre-senting his conceptions or opinions, he bestowed upon his interlocutors the transformative power of understanding through authentic self-reflection.

Socratic conversations rippled outward, touching the lives of Athenians in various strata of society, and leaving behind a legacy that would nourish the imagination of countless intellectuals to come.

The Socratic method goes beyond the realm of solely debunking claims or of unwinding fallacious logic. Instead, it shines as a powerful antidote to the inherent vulnerability of even the brightest minds to the ways our cognitive faculties betray us. It uncovers our implicit assumptions, prodding us to dig deeper into the roots of our convictions. By embracing this probing curiosity, Socrates embodied the quintessence of intellectual humility: the courage to not merely entertain uncertainties, but to dissect them with a surgeon's precision, to expose the naked truth beneath.

Socrates' commitment to relentless questioning transcended the particularities of ancient Athens and resonates throughout history. Indeed, the Socratic method has served as an enduring influence on education, pedagogy, and critical thinking. Its implications are sprawling, imbuing our pursuits of knowledge, morality, politics, and science with a spirit of self-awareness – and even self-doubt – that constantly spurs us to consider novel possibilities, revise our viewpoints, and seek wisdom in honest introspection.

However, the Socratic method's influence on key thinkers and intellectual movements cannot be separated from the more enigmatic aspects of Socrates' life. Born from this relentless questioning was a profusion of intellectual confrontations – with himself, the broader world, and those who held power within it. The Athenian democracy of the time was particularly susceptible to the revelatory force of his probing inquiries, as Socrates made no exceptions when it came to examining the foundations of power, just as one might scrutinize the precepts of geometry or the vicissitudes of nature.

These confrontations, though laden with an undeniable gravity, did not weigh him down. Rather, they illuminated the path, guiding him towards the truths he sought with such fervor. His dialogical encounters – as depicted in Plato's Socratic dialogues – bear witness to his unquenchable thirst for comprehending the world and human nature through a radically honest lens. It was through these conversations that he delved into the intricacies of ethics, epistemology, metaphysics, and other realms of philosophical delight.

Socrates' methodical dissection of traditional ideals and longstanding beliefs did not sit well with everyone. In fact, it posed a threat to those who wielded power and derived their authority from upholding the pillars of the status quo. By encouraging people to reassess and reflect upon their assumptions, Socrates likely elicited discomfort, as their dearly held convictions trembled under the weight of his probing questions. And yet, he pursued his quest for truth – a quest that led to his eventual prosecution.

Despite his untimely end, Socrates' relentless pursuit of truth through rigorous questioning of assumptions endures as a guiding light for subsequent generations of philosophers, thinkers, and truth-seekers. His unwavering dedication to intellectual humility and integrity has left an indelible mark on the pursuit of knowledge, inspiring us to scrutinize our conceptions, embrace uncertainty, and seek the wisdom of those who dare admit, "I don't know."

When one peers deeply into the life and teachings of Socrates, an intriguingly paradoxical theme unveils itself: his profound reluctance to claim possession of factual knowledge. It may seem counterintuitive for such a towering figure of intellectual history, one who elevated the importance of systematic interrogation, to embrace such an unassuming stance. Yet, as we come to understand more about the human predilection to cognitive error and fallacious reasoning, the subtlety of Socrates' stance starts to reveal itself as a potent force. Bordering on the subversive, his intellectual humility helped to forge a path that forever altered the landscape of Western philosophy and its pursuit of the truth.

A penetrating look into the essence of Socratic inquiry unveils the critical underpinnings of his refusal to assert any sense of certainty. To hold and propagate ideas without thorough examination was an affront to the very foundations of the Socratic method. This was not a passive resignation or dismissal of the value of knowledge and learning; on the contrary, he fervently sought to explore the nature of reality and wisdom itself. He did so not through promoting a specific dogma or set of beliefs, but by fostering an environment in which the compassionate crucible of scrutiny and reflection was the norm.

A remarkable testament to his reluctance to claim knowledge came in the form of his interactions with the Oracle of Delphi. The ancient priestess proclaimed that no one was wiser than Socrates himself, a claim that the great philosopher initially found baffling. Instead of allowing this declaration to amplify his intellectual authority or suppose he had somehow reached the pinnacle of wisdom, Socrates actively challenged the assertion. He took this as an opportunity to engage with individuals from various walks of life, seeking out that elusive kernel of knowledge that would contradict the Oracle's claim and prove he wasn't the wisest of men.

Yet, his pursuits led him to an unexpected and transformative revelation: the Oracle's assertion was indeed true, but not for reasons one might assume. Socrates' wisdom rested not on the possession of some immutable truths; rather, it sprouted from the fertile grounds of his humility and the constant recognition of his own ignorance. In an era colored by assumptions and caustic dogmatism, this humble insight emerged as a profound expression of self-awareness and the eternal search for wisdom – one that, to this day, shapes the contours of intellectual humility.

Socrates' sustained surrender to uncertainty underscored his unwavering belief that true wisdom resides in acknowledging the limits of one's own understanding. From the midst of philosophical inquiry's delicate interplay between dogmatism and doubt, Socrates crafted a philosophical compass that pointed steadfastly towards the ever-changing landscape of provisional knowledge. No matter how complex the terrain or profoundly life-altering the implications, he sought to examine it all fearlessly and without attachment to preconceived notions.

This conscious distancing from claims of expertise or dominion over truth laid the groundwork for a tradition that encouraged intellectual modesty – a spirit that echoed through centuries, inspiring numerous philosophers, scientists, and artists to immerse themselves in the seemingly ceaseless embrace of the unknown. They, like Socrates, sought wisdom not in the rote declaration of finite principles, but in the dynamic exploration of hypotheses and perspectives, forever striving for a richer understanding of the depths of human knowledge.

The aftershocks of the Socratic method, that intellectual wrestling with ideas in search of a nuanced understanding of the world, continue to reverberate through the ages. The principles that he championed—unyielding self-reflection, skeptical interrogation, and a deep-seated curiosity—cut a wide swath through Western philosophy, shaping great minds like Plato and Aristotle. And while Socrates never penned a single line, his legacy, etched across centuries through the written accounts of his contemporaries, endowed future generations with the indelible marks of his vibrant critical thinking. Ultimately, it is the palpable sense of inquisitive humility that permeates Socratic thought which remains his most enduring contribution to the realm of intellectual discourse.

To fully appreciate the extent of Socrates' impact on the philosophical tradition, we must cast our gaze toward those he directly influenced, starting with the perennial figure of his prized student, Plato. A resolute and prolific chronicler of Socrates' wisdom and methodology, Plato was perhaps the most receptive to the profound implications of his teacher's style and ideas. Through his extensive writings, many of which featured Socrates grappling with complex questions in engaging dialogues, Plato not only lent permanence to the ephemerality of verbal exchanges but also cultivated the spirit of inquiry that informed his own philosophical endeavors.

From the allegory of the cave to the theory of the forms, Plato's ideas have been interpreted and debated by countless scholars in manifold contexts, demonstrating the far-reaching consequences of a single teacher's intellectual influence. Socrates' spirit of inquiry, his restless pursuit of a deeper understanding of reality, subtly underscored Plato's grandest philosophical concepts, demonstrating the vitality of the interplay between teacher and student in the perpetuation of knowledge and the evolution of thought.

Following the lineage of the Socratic legacy, we encounter Aristotle, the eminent student of Plato. Although he would diverge from his teacher's thought in significant ways, Aristotle nonetheless stood on the shoulders of Socratic innovation. It is telling that despite their differences, the great philosophers of the day were bound by their common experience of grappling with Socrates' ideas and his pedagogical approach. Aristotle's substantial contributions to fields as diverse as ethics, politics, and natural philosophy owe, at least in part, to the intellectual ferment that permeated the era—a ferment born of the incandescent brilliance of Socrates and his revolutionary teaching methods.

Beyond the triumvirate of Socrates, Plato, and Aristotle, we see the emergence of intellectual traditions that diverge from the philosophical mainstream while still retaining a sincere acknowledgment of their Socratic origins. The teachings of the Cynics, for instance, sought to liberate humankind from the tyranny of social conventions, their commitment to interrogating societal norms standing as a testament to a shared lineage with Socrates. Similarly, the Stoics sought to inculcate a spirit of equanimity in their adherents, embracing a reflective ethos that found its roots in the deep humility of Socratic thought.

As we take note of these myriad connections, it becomes abundantly clear that the spirit of Socrates continues to wind its way through the sinewy annals of

Western philosophy. While the word "Socrates" may now conjure up images of a dialoguing old man in a toga, what truly endures is the ethos he lived and breathed: an unwavering curiosity, an abiding humility, and the voracious appetite for wisdom that defined him and those he inspired. Time and again, Socrates serves as a lodestar, guiding countless intellectual voyagers through the uncharted routes to truth that he so valiantly pioneered.

<h1 style="text-align:center">22</h1>

Charles Darwin and the unfolding truth of evolution

Another inscrutable figure lifting the veil of ignorance through the lens of intellectual humility, Charles Darwin, would go on to reshape not just the biological sciences but also the very human perception of our place within the world. Much like Socrates, Darwin's engagement with the enigma of life manifested an illumination that came from an acceptance of limits and exploration of the unknown. As we traverse the fascinating story of Darwin's life and his scientific accomplishments, the echoes of a Socratic outlook resound, establishing the notion that deep, lasting wisdom dwells not in grasping at certainty but through a relentless curiosity in the face of our own bounded comprehension.

Born in 1809 to a wealthy, well-connected family, Charles Darwin's early life seemed destined for mediocrity. His academic pursuits in medicine and theology did little to inspire him or to foreshadow the remarkable impact that he would go on to have on our understanding of life on Earth. However, as fate would have it, the opportunity to join a voyage aboard the HMS Beagle as a naturalist proffered Darwin the chance to explore the world beyond the imposed structure of formal academia. Over the next five years, his experience navigating distant realms and closely observing the remarkable diversity of plant and animal species lit the spark of revolutionary thought – one that would set the stage for scientific history.

As Darwin grappled with the confounding puzzle of the natural world and the intricate interconnections between life forms, his mind began formulating an explanatory structure to make sense of the complexity he found. The idea that life evolved slowly over millennia through small, incremental changes, driven by the pressures of natural selection, began to take firm root. This notion was radical and threatened to reshape the human understanding of our own origins and our relationship with the natural world entirely. Darwin recognized the weight of this idea and went to great lengths not to rush to any conclusions or proclamations. It took him twenty more years of meticulous observation, experimentation, and critical contemplation before the eventual completion of his magnum opus, On the Origin of Species.

Darwin's masterwork delineated the bold and groundbreaking framework of evolution and natural selection, shattering preconceived notions of the fixed, immutable nature of life on Earth. Fostering a holistic understanding of the interconnected tapestry that encompassed every living organism required a detailed examination of a multitude of species and their nuanced distinctions. The sheer depth and breadth of this inquiry necessitated a humility rarely found in scientific investigation, acknowledging not just the complexity of the world but also the inherent limitations in our ability to fully discern it. Darwin's exploration into evolution marked a monumental achievement, extending our grasp of the cosmic enigma of life into previously uncharted realms.

On the Origin of Species stands as a testament to the triumph of curiosity and circumspection over hubris and dogmatism. The manner in which Darwin unveiled his groundbreaking theory to the world reveals the delicate balance of courage and humility that is often necessary for progress. It is through dissecting these moments when humility governed his discourse that we can grasp the lasting implications of adopting such an approach within our own individual pursuits of truth.

Again, more than two decades of vigorous research prevailed before Darwin confidently put forth the theory of natural selection. This diligent pursuit of evidence and awareness of possible mistakes illuminates his commitment to intellectual integrity. Darwin's acknowledgment in On the Origin of Species that "long before having arrived at this part of my work, a crowd of difficulties will have occurred to the reader" displays an openness to apprehensions, a willingness to engage with potential shortcomings and inquiries that emerge from the scrutiny of his work.

Yet, perhaps the most resonant aspect of Darwin's intellectual humility was his ability to integrate numerous sources of knowledge – even when those sources made him question his own preconceptions. Darwin relentlessly corresponded with a wide array of experts in taxonomy, geology, comparative anatomy, and plant physiology. He readily acknowledged the contributions of his correspondents in his publications, claiming, "I hardly ever trust to the old observations which I made when the subject was not very clearly defined in my mind." This unwavering commitment to refining his thoughts by engaging with both his supporters and detractors stands as an exemplar of intellectual humility in action.

Darwin was also acutely aware that his theory had limits in his time. Even as the concept of evolution rapidly gained traction, he wrote, "Much light will be thrown on the origin of man and his history." His candid admission underscores his recognition that even his opus may not encompass the absolute truth but would instead inspire future generations to extend the boundaries of knowledge.

While submitting his manuscript, he expressed his fear that "all of us, will be in fleas' power very soon," highlighting his faith in the concept of evolution as an unfolding truth. He acknowledged the tentative and provisional nature of his work, always remaining cognizant that his ideas would be refined and developed by subsequent generations of scientists.

The humility that defined Darwin's approach to his work extends beyond assembling evidence and presenting it in On the Origin of Species. It is also evident in his agonizing personal struggle to reconcile the implications of his theory with the deeply held religious beliefs of his time, including those of his own wife, Emma. Darwin consciously navigated the dangerous waters of challenging long-held socio-religious perspectives with humility and delicacy, recognizing the fine line between pursuing truth and the sanctity of the beliefs held by those around him.

23

Albert Einstein's embrace of uncertainty in the universe

In the annals of human accomplishment, Albert Einstein occupies an enviable position – his name synonymous with genius, his face recognizable to an extraordinary range of people across the planet. His achievements in physics, particularly the theories of relativity – special and general – were to science what groundbreaking literature, art, and music were to culture. Yet, the underlying thread that wove Einstein's contributions together was not just a keen intellect, but also the presence of intellectual humility. This allowed him to transcend the confines of existing knowledge, challenge well-established theories, and embrace uncertainty. To comprehend the magnitude of his innovations, let us explore the constellation of his groundbreaking contributions to physics, and the context within which they emerged.

At the turn of the 20th century, physics was in a state of flux. The orderly and deterministic world proposed by Newtonian mechanics seemed inadequate to account for the rapidly emerging and confounding observations of the natural world at both the cosmological and subatomic levels. Enter the young Albert Einstein, unburdened by dogma and primed to question everything in his quest for understanding.

Einstein, in the early days of his career, wrestled with problems that perplexed physicists worldwide. One such problem was the incongruity between the absoluteness of space and time in classical mechanics and the invariance of electromagnetic phenomena under transformation. In the pursuit of a solution, he imagined the famous 'Gedankenexperiment' (thought experiment) of chasing a beam of light. This pursuit would uniquely coalesce, in 1905, into his Special Theory of Relativity. To the layperson, the theory may be shrouded in equations and subtleties, but at its core, it is an elegant portrait of the interdependence between time and space. By demonstrating that time and space were relative and dependent on an observer's state of motion, Einstein irrevocably changed the dimensions upon which we write the story of the universe.

The Special Theory of Relativity, however, was not the sole monument of Einstein's intellectual wanderings. That same year, in what has been dubbed his "Annus Mirabilis," or miraculous year, Einstein published other groundbreaking papers that revolutionized the way we understand the universe. Among these, one confronted the mysterious phenomenon of the photoelectric effect, wherein metals release electrons when illuminated by light of certain frequencies. With his deep intellectual curiosity and willingness to challenge entrenched assumptions, Einstein proposed that electromagnetic waves could behave as particles – later named photons – and their energy would be proportional to their frequency. This radical idea, which straddled the border between continuity and discontinuity, would provide the seedbed for the development of quantum mechanics and earn Einstein the Nobel Prize in Physics.

In the years that followed, as physicists around the world contended with the implications of Einstein's ideas, he himself grappled with a new challenge: reconciling his Special Theory of Relativity with the force that shapes the cosmos – gravity. By imagining an object held in place by the gravitational pull of Earth and contemplating what would happen if it were suddenly set free, Einstein found that the answer lay in the curvature of spacetime caused by the presence of massive objects. The realization that gravity was not just a force, but a result of the fundamental architecture of the universe, propelled Einstein to formulate his General Theory of Relativity.

Published in 1915, the General Theory of Relativity was a tour de force in theoretical physics, knitting together many avenues of inquiry that had seemed intractable. Its profound implications touched aspects of the physical world that had been hidden from human understanding for centuries. In an awe-inspiring synthesis of theory and observation, the general theory's predictions, such as the bending of light by gravity and gravitational redshift, were later confirmed with increasing precision, cementing Einstein's status as the vanguard of modern physics.

It is crucial to recognize that Einstein's achievements did not sprout forth in isolation. Indeed, each transformational step in his scientific journey occurred in vibrant dialogues with other thinkers and discoveries of his time. At the heart of this bustling intellectual ecosystem, Einstein stands as a figure of courageous curiosity, daring to look beyond the confines of established paradigms and embracing uncertainty during his relentless search for truth within the physical world.

Einstein's contributions to physics were not, however, confined to his theories of relativity or his work on the photoelectric effect. He also delved into the nascent field of quantum mechanics, the study of physics at the atomic and subatomic level, which stood at odds with his vision of a deterministic universe. In this new realm, brimming with uncertainty, Einstein's intellectual humility would be acutely tested.

The remarkable fusion of insights that formed Einstein's revolutionary contributions to physics is a testament to his prodigious intellect. However, it is also a chronicle of an evolving relationship with the concept of uncertainty and the limits of human understanding. In particular, his encounters with the nascent field of quantum mechanics exemplify the challenge of reconciling his convictions on the ordered nature of the universe with the intrinsically indeterminate principles of the quantum realm. To chart this journey, we venture into the turbulent intellectual landscape that shaped Einstein's reconciliation with quantum mechanics and the lessons it imparts on the embrace of uncertainty in the pursuit of knowledge.

In the early years of the 20th century, as Einstein's theories of relativity were gaining traction, another revolution was simmering at the frontiers of physics, dismantling the very foundations of classical mechanics and the deterministic worldview it propagated. Quantum mechanics, born out of the efforts of brilliant minds like Max Planck, Niels Bohr, Werner Heisenberg, and Erwin Schrödinger, to name a few, sought to grapple with the seemingly irreconcilable behavior of particles at the atomic and subatomic levels. Through a series of groundbreaking experiments, they unveiled a realm where the neat deterministic laws of classical physics appeared to dissolve into an indeterminate landscape of probabilities. It was a world that defied human intuition, where particles danced between states of being and wavered in the realm of possibility – a world haunted by the specter of uncertainty.

Amid this paradigmatic upheaval, Einstein found himself confronted by the dissonance between the principles of quantum mechanics and his convictions about the harmony and determinism intrinsic to the universe. He regarded quantum mechanics as logically incomplete and, in his famous correspondence with Max Born, the physicist and close friend, he wrote, "Quantum mechanics is very impressive. But an inner voice tells me that it is not yet the real thing." This sentiment, coursing through Einstein's response to the nascent field, led him to embark on a lifelong quest to refine, challenge, and reconcile quantum mechanics with his broader vision of reality.

At the heart of this tension was the principle of wave-particle duality, which stipulated that particles like electrons or photons could exhibit both wave-like and particle-like behaviors, depending on how they were observed. This disparate existence, propagated by the growing body of experimental evidence, jostled with Einstein's deeply entrenched belief in the linear, deterministic nature of physical phenomena. For Einstein, the stochastic interpretations of quantum theory seemed to be a too-convenient obfuscation of a deeper, hidden order.

In an attempt to unearth this elusive order and disentangle the mysteries of quantum mechanics, Einstein turned to thought experiments – the very method that had served him so well in his development of relativity. Chief among these was his critique of the uncertainty principle proposed by Werner Heisenberg, which posited that it was fundamentally impossible to precisely know both the position and momentum of a particle simultaneously. Einstein, unwilling to accept this apparent limitation of knowledge, devised a thought experiment wherein a couple of particles interacted, and their properties were correlated – a scenario that would later, albeit unknowingly, lay the groundwork for the development of quantum entanglement.

Einstein's tireless inquiries into the principles of quantum mechanics were not for naught. They not only fueled a spirited debate with Heisenberg and Bohr but also contributed to the development of the subtler aspects of quantum theory. Among his most famous critiques was the EPR paradox, named for its authors, Einstein, Boris Podolsky, and Nathan Rosen, which sought to expose the perceived weaknesses in the concept of quantum entanglement. The EPR paradox challenged the establishment by presenting a scenario where two entangled particles, separated by vast distances, could instantaneously influence one another, seemingly violating the prohibition on faster-than-light communication dictated by Einstein's own Special Theory of Relativity. This enigmatic behavior came to be known as "spooky action at a distance," and it served as the crux of Einstein's dissent regarding the completeness of quantum mechanics.

However, Einstein's challenges to the dominant narrative did not end with the EPR paradox. In the decades that followed, the interplay between his critiques and the burgeoning field of quantum mechanics would shepherd the discipline towards deeper insights and a more mature understanding of the fundamental nature of reality. This iterative process, punctuated by Einstein's debates with luminaries like Bohr and Born, underscored the value of intellectual humility in an age of paradigm shifts and uncertainty. Even as he resisted the implications of quantum mechanics, Einstein was, in essence, honing the theories of his contemporaries, pushing the boundaries of knowledge, and proving that the intellectual struggle is, in itself, a beacon of scientific progress.

As we reflect upon Einstein's odyssey through the perplexing realm of quantum mechanics, it is vital to acknowledge the extraordinary resilience and curiosity that propelled him forward. The story of his reconciliation with this new, probabilistic worldview underscores the importance of intellectual humility and adaptability amid uncertainty – whether we stride across the limitless expanse of the cosmos or delve deep into the enigmatic heart of the atom.

In our quest to examine the seemingly paradoxical nature of human intelligence, wherein breathtaking discoveries coexist alongside inexplicable errors in judgment, we now turn our gaze towards the role of uncertainty within Einstein's own theoretical framework. It may come as a surprise to many that someone who initially resisted acknowledging the inherent indeterminacy in quantum mechanics – a theory that stood in stark contrast to the deterministic framework of classical physics – would go on to develop groundbreaking theories with uncertainty at their very core. The exploration of this fascinating interplay between certainty and uncertainty in Einstein's life's work illumines the importance of embracing intellectual humility and adaptability when navigating the ever-shifting boundaries of our understanding.

To truly appreciate the presence of uncertainty in Einstein's theories, we must first revisit the conceptual underpinnings of his most influential contributions – the Special Theory of Relativity and the General Theory of Relativity. At their essence, both theories address the fundamental nature of space, time, and gravitation, redefining our understanding of the cosmos and reshaping the course of modern physics in the process. However, as we shall see, these revolutionary ideas deftly incorporate elements of uncertainty that force us to reassess our relation to the universe and the limits of our comprehension.

The Special Theory of Relativity, published in 1905, posits a scenario in which the laws of physics remain consistent across all inertial (non-accelerating) frames of reference, with the speed of light being the same regardless of an observer's relative motion. This revolutionary postulate, when combined with Einstein's observations of time dilation and length contraction, partially dismantled the long-held belief in the absolute nature of space and time. In effect, the newfound understanding was that the temporal and spatial dimensions were relative and dependent on an observer's frame of reference, thus introducing an intrinsic measure of uncertainty to any assessment of spatial location or duration.

Einstein's General Theory of Relativity, unveiled in 1915, expanded upon these findings, weaving a rich narrative on the interplay of space, time, and gravitation. In this explanatory framework, the seemingly inflexible stage, upon which the meticulously ordered events of the cosmos had once transpired, was replaced by a malleable fabric of spacetime that curved and flexed under the influence of mass and energy. This transformative illustration of reality highlighted that any attempt at understanding the workings of the universe must inherently contend with the fluctuating nature of spacetime itself, further underscoring the undetachable presence of uncertainty within our appraisal of physical phenomena.

As the implications of Einstein's theories of relativity began to reverberate throughout the scientific community, numerous thinkers embarked upon their own journeys to grapple with the newfound uncertainty inherent in our understanding of the cosmos. One such mind was Werner Heisenberg, whose development of the uncertainty principle – the notion that it is fundamentally impossible to precisely know both the position and momentum of a particle at the same time – would once again redefine the limits of our knowledge. Although Heisenberg's proposal initially met with resistance from Einstein, it ultimately highlighted another intriguing layer of uncertainty embedded within the fabric of reality.

Moreover, Einstein's General Theory of Relativity paved the way for our current understanding of the expanding nature of the universe, which, during his time, stood in opposition to the prevailing belief in a static cosmos. In recognizing the inherent expansion at the heart of the universe's structure, Einstein laid the foundation for the subsequent discovery of the cosmic microwave background radiation – a finding that strengthened the case for the Big Bang Theory and the extraordinary notion of a universe born from an infinitesimally small, dense, and hot singularity. The very genesis of the universe, inextricably entwined with the uncertain, shifting values of space, time, and energy, further demonstrated that the pursuit of knowledge, even on a cosmic scale, must embrace the inherent vagaries and indeterminacy that define our existence.

In examining the role of uncertainty within Einstein's theories, we are not only reminded of the intrinsic limits of our knowledge but also of the importance of intellectual humility in the face of the unknown. Through his groundbreaking insights, Einstein deftly illustrated the intricate dance between certainty and uncertainty, demonstrating that the two contrasting forces are not only natural partners but also crucial elements in the expansion of our awareness.

In reflection, while it may at first seem ironic that Einstein – the very figure who would come to develop theories characterized by their intrinsic embrace of uncertainty – initially resisted the indeterminate principles of quantum mechanics, his journey towards acceptance serves as a testament to the necessity for adaptability and openness in the pursuit of knowledge.

As we continue to trace the arc of Einstein's life, it is essential to reimagine the context in which his groundbreaking theories emerged. At the outset of the 20th century, the scientific landscape was rife with opportunity and challenge: the advent of X-rays, the puzzling nature of radiation, and the mysterious properties of the electron fueled an intense fervor for discovery. Scientists and philosophers alike grappled with the implications of these new findings, prompting heated debates on the nature of reality and the very essence of existence.

It is within this transforming milieu that Einstein astutely navigated, propelled by his insatiable inquisitiveness and deep-seated conviction in the transcendent power of the imagination. Albert once declared, "I have no special talents. I am only passionately curious," suggesting that his remarkable intellect was intimately intertwined with his indefatigable quest for understanding. Indeed, what set Einstein apart was not his inherent genius alone, but rather the combination of his extraordinary abilities with an unwavering commitment to exploration, discovery, and growth.

In reflecting on Einstein's trajectory – from a disenchanted young student struggling in the traditional education system to a visionary physicist and global icon – we can discern several key components that contributed to his adaptive prowess. Primarily, Einstein's deep-seated intellectual curiosity propelled him to question entrenched beliefs, assumptions, and orthodoxies in favor of forging new paths to knowledge. This curiosity, coupled with humility in acknowledging the limitations of our comprehension, allowed Einstein to examine problems from fresh angles and envision novel solutions that expanded the realm of the possible.

One striking demonstration of Einstein's adaptability was his ability to contend with paradox and contradiction in the unfolding course of scientific inquiry. As a young thinker, he was captivated by the influential work of his predecessors such as Isaac Newton and James Clerk Maxwell, whose theories guided physicists' understanding of the universe. However, Einstein's growing recognition of the limitations in the classical paradigm led him to devise innovative theoretical frameworks that both built upon and transcended the contributions of those who came before.

Even within his own theories, Einstein displayed a remarkable capacity to adapt his thinking and embrace change. In the development of his General Theory of Relativity, Einstein later acknowledged an error he had made in including the cosmological constant – a mathematical term intended to preserve the notion of a static universe, which was the prevailing belief at the time. Through his willingness to revise his understanding and entertain the possibility of a dynamically evolving cosmos, Einstein demonstrated an insightful awareness that new insights call for continuous refinement and adaptation of previously held convictions.

Another cornerstone of Einstein's adaptive approach to scientific inquiry was his steadfast commitment to empirical evidence. Often guided by his intuitive sense of the world, Einstein nevertheless recognized that intuition alone was insufficient to propel our understanding of the universe forward. In the wake of his theoretical advances, crucial experimental work – such as Arthur Eddington's observations of stellar deflections during a solar eclipse – served to corroborate and bolster Einstein's insights.

This unwavering respect for empirical data would later play a significant role in Einstein's evolving stance on quantum mechanics – a theory whose indeterminate principles originally struck him as counterintuitive and irreconcilable with the laws governing macroscopic phenomena. As compelling experimental evidence mounted in support of the quantum paradigm, Einstein gradually embraced the theory's inherent uncertainty, displaying a remarkable intellectual flexibility and openness to new perspectives.

Einstein's journey also highlights the importance of fostering interdisciplinary connections and nurturing intellectual communities that inspire curiosity, critical thinking, and creative problem-solving. Through his engagement with the various intellectual circles in which he participated – such as the Olympia Academy and the Solvay Conferences – Einstein engaged in transformative dialogues that fostered the cross-pollination of ideas and facilitated breakthroughs in multiple scientific domains.

Taken together, these facets of Einstein's life and work coalesce to underscore a central message that resonates throughout our exploration of human intelligence and adaptability: that the path to wisdom and enlightenment is forged not by the complacent acceptance of established knowledge, but rather through the arduous pursuit of discovery, the courage to challenge prevailing dogma, and the humility to embrace uncertainty. In celebrating Einstein's journey, we are reminded of the enduring power of adaptability and intellectual humility, fortified by an indomitable spirit in the face of life's ever-changing landscape. As we continue to grapple with the complex tapestry of human intelligence and the dynamic interplay between genius and fallibility, we stand to learn much from the inquisitive and innovative approach that characterized Einstein's foray into the vast unknown.

24

Mahatma Gandhi and the power of intellectual humility in peace and conflict resolution

In this next chapter of our exploration, we shift our lenses to focus on the life and philosophy of another luminary who has left an indelible mark on the course of human history: Mahatma Gandhi. Just as Einstein's pursuit of truth illuminated the vast cosmos and the nature of reality, Gandhi's relentless devotion to truth-seeking – or satyagraha, as he termed it – unveiled a new horizon of possibility for humanity. A horizon in which peace, compassion, and dignity hold sway over injustice, violence, and oppression.

Gandhi's life was by no means a linear trajectory of grand accomplishments. Instead, it was a meandering path, strewn with trials and tribulations, moments of deep introspection, and ceaseless personal growth – a journey that ultimately chiseled him into the iconic figure we have come to revere today. As we embark on this exploration, it is essential to appreciate the rich and nuanced tapestry of influences, relationships, and experiences that informed Gandhi's evolving worldview and fueled his unwavering pursuit of justice.

Born in 1869 to a modest family in the small town of Porbandar, situated along the western coast of India, Mohandas Karamchand Gandhi was in many ways an unlikely candidate for leading the struggle for India's independence. For much of his youth and early adulthood, Gandhi was marked by an acute shyness, diffidence, and introspection – far from the qualities one might ordinarily associate with the transformative leaders of history.

Yet within this reticent young man, there laid a spark – a quiet determination to challenge the confines of his upbringing and forge his identity within the broader world. This early determination led him to embark on a journey across continents – from studying law in England to cutting his teeth as a legal practitioner in South Africa. It was during his time in South Africa that Gandhi's transformative experiences of racial discrimination planted the seeds of his social and political awakening – an awakening that would eventually catalyze a global movement for civil rights, justice, and equality.

As we chart the course of Gandhi's spiritual and philosophical development, several formative influences emerge as instrumental in shaping his outlook on the world and the nature of truth. One such influence was the spiritual heritage of his native India, which instilled in him a keen sense of interconnectedness, karma, and the transcendent power of love and compassion. This deep grounding in the ancient wisdom of the East was complemented by his voracious engagement with Western thought and literature.

Gandhi's affinity for the works of Western thinkers such as Thoreau, Emerson, and Tolstoy demonstrated his openness to cross-cultural exchanges of ideas and an abiding curiosity that transcended the boundaries of tradition and geography. Indeed, elements of these thinkers' philosophies, particularly their emphasis on individual conscience, nonviolence, and moral responsibility, would come to play a significant role in shaping Gandhi's own beliefs and convictions.

As we peel back the layers of Gandhi's philosophical evolution, we encounter an intricate mosaic of beliefs and ideas – a mosaic that reflects a constant striving to unearth the deeper currents of meaning beneath the surface of human existence. From his early attraction to the principles of Jainism – an ancient Indian faith that extols the virtues of nonviolence, or ahimsa – to his profound empathy for humanity's shared struggles and aspirations, Gandhi sought to synthesize the diverse threads of his intellectual journey into a coherent and inspiring vision of life.

At the heart of Gandhi's philosophical edifice lies the concept of satyagraha – an innovative approach to social and political change that harnesses the power of truth and nonviolence to combat injustice and oppression. Derived from the Sanskrit words for "truth" (satya) and "holding firmly" (agraha), satyagraha is an intricate and adaptive strategy that defies simplistic categorization. Yet, beneath its manifold manifestations lies a foundational commitment to love, compassion, and a belief in the ultimate triumph of truth over falsehood.

Gandhi's development and application of satyagraha was not merely a matter of intellectual abstraction; it was forged in the crucible of real-life experiences and personal sacrifice. Over the course of his life, Gandhi spearheaded numerous nonviolent campaigns aimed at alleviating racial injustice in South Africa and securing India's independence from British rule, often facing considerable opposition and hardship in the process.

In his pursuit of peace and justice, Gandhi often faced powerful adversaries. Yet in these moments of confrontation, he proved adept at deploying a strategy he termed "heart-unity" – an approach that emphasized human connection and the power of empathy to overcome divisiveness and antagonism. As we shall see, this pursuit of heart-unity not only yielded concrete results in the form of political and social progress, but also demonstrated the profound impact of intellectual humility as both a means and an end in the service of human flourishing.

Building upon the moral foundation of ahimsa and the intellectual humility that defined Gandhi's life and thought, we can now turn our attention to the practical strategies and methods he employed in his fight for justice and equality. Rooted in compassion and a burning desire to alleviate the suffering of his fellow human beings, Gandhi's nonviolent resistance campaigns signaled a transformative shift in the nature of political activism, demonstrating the power of principled restraint in swaying public opinion and effecting lasting social change. By examining these strategies, we can glean valuable insights into the process of promoting peace and reconciliation in even the most contentious of conflicts.

One of the most distinctive and innovative elements of Gandhi's approach to nonviolent resistance is his understanding of the interconnectedness of violence in its myriad forms, from the visceral to the structural. This holistic awareness of violence led him to develop a two-pronged strategy for addressing both its overt manifestations, such as colonialism and violence between religious or ethnic groups, as well as the more subtle and insidious forms of exploitation that pervade social and economic systems. From the British-imposed salt taxes to the catastrophic consequences of industrialization on rural tradespeople, Gandhi was attuned to the diverse sufferings that lay beneath the surface of everyday life, and he sought to address these inequities through his nonviolent campaigns.

To challenge systemic injustice and create a more equitable society, Gandhi devised a multi-layered approach that encompassed personal reflection and dedication, community engagement, and large-scale political activism. Starting with the individual, he espoused a philosophy of self-sufficiency and self-control as the backbone of nonviolent resistance. This emphasis on personal discipline equipped his followers with the fortitude to withstand the aggression and harassment they often faced in the course of their activism.

At the community level, Gandhi encouraged the cultivation of deep, empathetic relationships between people of different cultural, religious, and societal backgrounds. He organized meetings, rallies, and other events that brought these diverse groups together, fostering mutual understanding and a shared sense of purpose. Through these gatherings, Gandhi helped to dissolve the barriers that separated people from one another, forging a collective identity that transcended the divisions that had long perpetuated violence and injustice.

Solidarity and collaboration emerged as cornerstones of Gandhi's larger-scale political activism, which hinged on his ability to mobilize disparate segments of the Indian population against the injustices of British colonial rule. These methods of mass resistance included civil disobedience—a powerful, passive form of protest that involved defying unjust laws or policies, often at great personal risk. Civil disobedience enabled ordinary Indians to participate in a shared struggle against oppression while maintaining the principles of nonviolence and compassion at the forefront of their activism.

One of Gandhi's most famous and successful acts of civil disobedience was the Salt March of 1930, which challenged British salt taxation and highlighted the colonial government's exploitation of India's natural resources. By leading a 240-mile march to the Arabian Sea and deliberately violating the British salt monopoly, Gandhi galvanized a national movement that awakened a new spirit of collective determination among the Indian people. Though the immediate material gains of the Salt March were limited, the campaign struck a powerful symbolic blow against the British colonial regime and further proved the effectiveness of nonviolent resistance strategies.

Another crucial element of Gandhi's nonviolent resistance was his practice of fasting, which he employed on numerous occasions to bring attention to specific conflicts and injustices. By voluntarily undergoing substantial hardship and pain, Gandhi sought to inspire his followers to reevaluate their own behavior and choices in the face of suffering. Through these acts of self-imposed deprivation, Gandhi not only demonstrated his personal commitment to the principles of nonviolence and truth-seeking but also fostered a sense of unity and shared purpose among his fellow activists.

One notable example of Gandhi's use of fasting as a political tool occurred in response to the violence and unrest surrounding India's negotiations for independence in 1947. As the British government prepared to transfer power to the soon-to-be-divided India and Pakistan, communal violence erupted between Hindus, Muslims, and Sikhs. Deeply disturbed by these developments, Gandhi went on a fast in protest against the bloodshed and pledged to maintain his abstinence until peace was restored. In this moment of crisis, Gandhi's fast proved to be a profoundly potent symbol of his dedication to nonviolent principles and became a rallying cry for the nation to seek a peaceful resolution to the conflict.

As we have now delved into the key strategies and tactics that undergirded Gandhi's nonviolent resistance campaigns, it becomes clear how these methods served to both challenge and transform the societies and systems they targeted. By developing a comprehensive approach that addressed individuals' personal choices, local community dynamics, and larger political structures, Gandhi illustrated the potential for nonviolence to serve as a potent force for change in a complex, often tumultuous world.

Moreover, in practicing and promoting nonviolent resistance, Gandhi demonstrated that the pursuit of justice need not be predicated on aggression or domination, but rather on a fundamental commitment to compassion and truth-seeking. His unwavering dedication to these principles, combined with his pragmatic, adaptive approach to confronting the challenges of his time, offers us a powerful model for navigating our contemporary struggles in a way that preserves our humanity and upholds the intrinsic value of all lives.

Throughout his life, Gandhi demonstrated an unwavering commitment to intellectual humility, the willingness to acknowledge one's own limitations and remain open to the perspectives and experiences of others. By upholding this principle in his beliefs, actions, and campaigns, Gandhi effectively ignited a transformative process that not only spurred India's struggle for independence but also inspired a myriad of movements worldwide. This humble approach to activism and change offers a powerful alternative to confrontational tactics and provides a roadmap for how we might navigate the challenges we face today.

Intellectual humility, at its core, is the antithesis of dogmatism, the rigid adherence to one's beliefs, typically resulting from overconfidence or un-willingness to accept the possibility of being wrong. By contrast, intellectual humility recognizes that human knowledge is finite, constantly evolving, and subject to revision in light of new information or insights. Embracing this principle allows for a more inclusive, empathetic, and ultimately more effective approach to crafting societal change.

In the context of Gandhi's work and philosophy, intellectual humility manifested itself in numerous ways, from his commitment to engaging in dialogue with opponents to his emphasis on self-discipline and introspection. Throughout the breadth of his political activism, Gandhi maintained a fervent belief that acknowledging one's own limitations and incorporating the lessons learned from others was a necessary component for achieving change.

One of the ways in which Gandhi operationalized intellectual humility in his pursuit of a just society was through his commitment to fostering dialogue and debate, both at the individual and collective level. He consistently engaged in discussions with a wide range of people, including his allies, adversaries, and even the British colonial rulers. By exposing himself to diverse perspectives and grappling with complex ideas, Gandhi was able to cultivate a deeper understanding of the issues he sought to address and devise more effective strategies for advocating change.

Take, for example, his interactions with the British, who remained his political adversaries throughout his struggle for India's independence. Despite being in direct opposition to their ultimate goals, Gandhi persistently engaged in discussions with various British officials, striving to understand their point of view, and fostering a sense of mutual respect. This approach not only opened up space for dialogue and negotiation between the two sides but also demonstrated to the Indian people the power of intellectual humility in driving social and political change.

Gandhi's commitment to intellectual humility was not limited to his interactions with others but also extended to the realm of self-reflection and personal growth. He maintained an ongoing process of examining his own beliefs and reassessing the strategies he employed in his activism. For instance, after several of his campaigns resulted in violence or unintended consequences, Gandhi called for a period of reflection and self-critique, admitting that mistakes had been made and urging his fellow activists to pause and reassess their approach.

This willingness to adapt and evolve in response to new information or experiences exemplifies the intellectual humility that permeated Gandhi's entire philosophy. Amid the tumultuous landscape of India's struggle for independence, his ability to remain steadfastly open to critique and the possibility of his own fallibility presented a powerful example of how intellectual humility could be harnessed as a force for societal change and growth.

Beyond his personal actions and encounters, Gandhi's approach to intellectual humility had a profound impact on the broader Indian independence movement. By espousing a philosophy based on humble inquiry and the willingness to learn from others, Gandhi nurtured a culture of inclusion and collaboration while also challenging the divisive forces that threatened to tear the Indian subcontinent apart. Through his humble leadership style, Gandhi influenced generations of activists to engage in constructive dialogue, actively seeking out a diversity of perspectives in pursuit of a more just society.

The long-lasting impact of Gandhi's intellectual humility cannot be over-stated, as numerous social and political movements have since drawn inspiration from his philosophy and strategies. From the American civil rights movement, championed by leaders like Martin Luther King Jr., to the anti-apartheid struggle in South Africa, guided by Nelson Mandela, Gandhi's commitment to intellectual humility and nonviolent resistance has left an indelible mark on the global landscape of activism and change.

As we grapple with the myriad challenges and conflicts that define our contemporary world, it is worth reflecting on the transformative potential of intellectual humility as embodied in the life and work of Mahatma Gandhi. By embracing the wisdom of admitting ignorance, fostering open dialogue, and maintaining a steadfast commitment to empathy, we can begin to chart a path towards a more compassionate, inclusive, and ultimately, more just society. The lessons gleaned from Gandhi's nonviolent activism and his dedication to intellectual humility serve as a powerful reminder of the inherent value in cultivating our own capacity for understanding, self-awareness, and adaptability.

IV

The Elusive Nature of Truth and the Importance of Provisional Knowledge

25

What is truth? An exploration of various philosophical perspectives

Having delved deeply into the cognitive hurdles that impede our judgment and the innumerable benefits of adopting intellectual humility, as exemplified in the life and work of Mahatma Gandhi, it is now time for us to confront an even greater challenge: engaging with the elusive nature of truth itself. From the early philosophers who vigorously debated the nature of reality to modern scientists unraveling the rules which govern the universe, humankind has ceaselessly attempted to discern the nature of truth in all its forms.

We have encountered divergent ideologies and seemingly contradictory conclusions, often leading to situations where no definitive solution seems apparent. In order to navigate these ill-defined waters, we have come to rely heavily on provisional truths, which aptly reflect our evolving understanding of the world around us. Intellectual humility encourages us to grasp this concept of provisional truth, aiding in the flexible adaptation of our beliefs based on changing information or newly acquired knowledge.

Let us first be reminded of the words of the famed philosopher Socrates, who once claimed that "the only thing that I know is that I know nothing." From Socrates' provocative statement, we can begin to understand the indelible link between intellectual humility and the precarious nature of truth itself. Although few would claim to possess comprehensive knowledge of truth, it is this willingness to admit our vulnerability, the candid acceptance of the limits of our understanding, which allows us to open our minds and explore new terrains of thought.

It is crucial to recognize that our understanding of truth is not limited to scientific advancements or philosophical musings alone. Instead, the quest for truth traverses the vast landscapes of human endeavor, incorporating our emotional experiences and intuitive inclinations as well as any empirical evidence we may gather.

To navigate the labyrinthine dimensions of truth, we must first acknowledge the factors that contribute to its formation. Truth is often perceived as an objective quality, a firm and unchanging aspect of reality that, once discovered, can be relied upon indefinitely. In reality, this notion of truth as an unyielding structure is, in itself, a fallacy. For it is only through the lens of our understanding of the world, which is as complex and multifaceted as the individuals who inhabit it, that we interpret these alleged truisms.

As we excavate deeper into the realm of truth, it becomes abundantly clear that truth is as heavily influenced by our senses as it is by our reasoning. Our tactile experiences provide us with impressions of reality, a ceaseless flow of data which our minds then attempt to arrange into coherent constructs – what we call "truth." At times, this process is a seamless and efficient interplay between sensory inputs and intellectual synthesis, resulting in clear and accurate depictions of our surroundings. However, more frequently than not, our perceptions are blemished by imprecision, falsehood, and bias – demonstrating, once again, the importance of approaching truth with intellectual humility.

Let us consider the tantalizing question: Is there a singular, universal definition of truth to which we can reliably tether ourselves? Or, much like our innate cognitive idiosyncrasies, is truth a multi-layered and fluctuating entity – one that exists innumerable shapes and shades and can be illuminated or obscured by the shifting relics of a fleeting world?

In an attempt to answer these questions, scholars and philosophers across the ages have crafted a panoply of theories, each encapsulating their own particular approach to dissecting the enigma of truth. These perspectives, which we will now explore, serve as essential equipment on our journey down this uncharted path. They provide not only a necessary contextual framework for our exploration of truth but also bear testimony to the vast expanse of human thought that has grappled with the notion of truth since time immemorial.

It is worth noting that these dialogues and theories concerning truth emerged from distinct cultural, religious, and historical contexts. Ancient civilizations, such as the Egyptians and the Chinese, perceived truth as innately connected to moral and ethical considerations, a notion that persists in various iterations today. The rich traditions of Indian philosophy, on the other hand, offer an intriguing juxtaposition between the search for absolute truth (paramārtha-satya) and the recognition of relative or conventional truth (saṃvṛti-satya).

We begin our exploration of the correspondence theory of truth by observing the core tenet upon which it rests: that there is a deep and intrinsic connection between our beliefs, thoughts, and the outside world that substantiates their veracity. Often considered the most intuitive and widely-held perspective on truth, its allure lies in its seemingly evident simplicity. The essence of the correspondence theory suggests that our concepts and beliefs resonate to outside reality, like vast orchestras tuning themselves to the pitch of the world in which we exist.

In their attempt to elucidate the correspondence theory, our forerunners have regarded truth as correspondence between the statements we form and their counterparts in reality. As we navigate through the realm of all possible descriptions of the world, we find those which are congruent with the world's goings-on, those which seem to mirror the facets of reality that we perceive, and we call them truthful. Similarly, those descriptions that find no match within the contours of the world's fabric are cast into the abyss of falsehood.

Aristotle, who played a critical role in shaping our understanding of this theory, posited that when our thoughts align with reality—when, for example, we believe that the sun is shining and it is, indeed, sunny—we embody truth. Conversely, when our beliefs contravene the tenets of the outside world, we usher into existence the province of untruth. It is this elementary notion of truth, as a symbolic connection between the world and our comprehension of it, that forms the cornerstone of the correspondence theory.

Proponents of this theory argue that truth is contingent upon accuracy—the extent to which our beliefs sync with the rhythms of the external world. This principle has an undeniable appeal for those who wish to ground themselves in the world's unwavering physicality. It is the bedrock that preserves our connection with a tangible reality, while simultaneously undermining the very foundations of relativism and unrestrained subjectivity.

Despite its allure, the correspondence theory is not without its critics. Opponents argue that this picture of truth may be misleadingly simplistic, relying on the assumption that the terrain of reality is knowable in its entirety. They caution that the metaphorical map we create to understand the world is, necessarily, colored by the lenses through which we see it. The tapestry we weave to encapsulate our comprehension of the external world may be susceptible to a distortion—a warping, a stretching, or a fraying—by the very fabric of our unique human experience.

For some, these limitations provoke a challenge, one that seeks to unearth the true nature of correspondence and to expand its horizons beyond the outer boundaries of thought. One such scholar is the esteemed Bertrand Russell, an intellectual titan who, like Socrates and Darwin before him, embraced humility in his pursuit of truth. Russell postulated that our minds forge representations to typify the kaleidoscope of the world around us, and that these facsimiles might reorient and adapt to ensure a closer correspondence with the landscapes they symbolize.

However, Russell's inquiries sparked a consequential and, for some, disquieting revelation: a realization that representation itself can be an inherently imprecise endeavor, one that is necessarily filtered through our human faculties. The warnings of Plato's allegory of the cave echo through the millennia as a potent caution against overconfidence in our perceptions.

Tucked within the pages of Plato's renowned work "The Republic," we discover one of the most potent allegories of Western philosophy. Plato presents a tale that explores the deep chasm between perception and reality, challenging the foundations of our knowledge and calling into question the unanimity of our truths. It's a journey from gross illusion to uncomfortable knowledge, from the shackles of ignorance to the freedom of enlightenment, and importantly, from the realm of shadows to the world of light.

In the allegory, Plato devises a world where individuals have been held captive since infancy inside a large hollow cave with an entrance facing the bright light of the world beyond. These prisoners live in perpetual confinement, shackled in a manner that restricts their movement and only allows them to look at the wall ahead. Behind them is a fire, operated by puppeteers who parade a range of objects across the stage of the cave in front of the fire—the shadows of which are cast onto the opposite wall within the prisoners' sight.

These shadows, ephemeral and devoid of real substance, constitute the entirety of the prisoners' reality. They've never experienced the world outside the cave, so they take these shadows as their only truth. They debate, speculate, and form hierarchies over who is the most adroit at predicting the sequence in which these shadows appear and vanish. For them, reality lies entirely within the walls of their darkened dwelling, their understanding limited to the ghostly echoes that reverberate around the cave.

But consider a scenario pressed forth by Plato's imagination where one of these prisoners is freed, complicit only in confronting the ignis fatuus of his erstwhile existence. Initially, the surge of light hurts his eyes, and the brilliance of the world beyond the cave baffles him. The objects he once recognized only as shadows are now substantiated into a vivacious array of colors, shapes, and forms. He struggles to reconcile with reality, for it far surpasses the prosaic record of shadows he had mindlessly memorized back in the cave.

This emancipated prisoner experiences an epiphany, a resurgence of clarity, upon realizing the shadows' reality: They are mere illusions, impoverished representations of the vibrant world that traces its existence to the sun's radiant glow. After basking in this revelation, a profound consciousness shifts within the freed man—an expanded awareness awakens him to a truth far removed from his former ignorance and illusions.

The flickering shadows that dance upon the cave's walls serve as a stark reminder of the deceptive character of perception and the extent to which our beliefs can languish in the darkness of falsehood.

Let us not, though, abandon hope for the correspondence theory or collapse under the weight of its perceived shortcomings. Instead, we can adopt a stance of intellectual humility and acknowledge that the world is replete with subtleties, ambiguities, and complexities which at times baffle and elude even our most adroit reasoning. Moreover, we can fill the reservoir of our knowledge with the wisdom of the correspondence theory proponents, like Russell, who remind us that correspondence itself transcends the rigidity of a simple one-to-one conformity with external phenomena.

Emboldened by this realization, we can procure the tools required to strain the legibility of the shadows on the cave's walls. As we peer cautiously into the darkness, we can reevaluate our approach to discerning truth through correspondence, gingerly embracing its elasticity as our minds struggle to make sense of the vast expanse that stretches before them.

In unearthing the symbolic links that tether words and meaning, we gain a deeper understanding of correspondence and can better appreciate the powerful potential it holds. Ultimately, correspondence theory offers us a framework for aligning our beliefs with the infinite complexity and diversity of the world—one that, with our awareness of its limitations, endorses an attitude of flexibility, curiosity and, above all, intellectual humility.

Consider now, having embarked on our journey from the grounding acquaintance of the correspondence theory, we find ourselves confronting a different perspective, an orientation that seeks to discover truth not in the contours of an external reality but within the network of our own beliefs—the Coherence theory of truth. This perspective prescribes that a statement holds truth not because it mirrors the outer world, but because it consistently fits within a broader system of beliefs or knowledge: it coheres.

At the crux of the Coherence theory lies a tenet of mutual reinforcement. Imagine a web of beliefs, where each strand is an assertion or perspective. Some may be strong, established through repeated validation and reinforced by their interconnectedness with other strands. Others may be weaker, their affiliations tenuous, their substantiation debatable.

If we were to introduce a new belief into this already bustling web, we would not measure its truth by aligning it to a physical manifestation in the real world. Instead, its truthfulness would be tested through the harmony it shares with the existing structures, by the extent to which it interweaves with, buttresses, and is buttressed by the existing strands of the web.

The philosopher Brand Blanshard, in illustrating the Coherence theory, paints a picture not dissimilar to our analogy of the web. He imagines our system of beliefs as a vast and intricately interlinked network, a sort of intellectual structure wherein each component part, each belief, must bear the weight of coherence with every other.

It's a conception of truth that turns inwards, placing less emphasis on an external, objective reality and instead prioritizes the overall harmony of our beliefs and assumptions. Unlike the austere correspondence theory—which, remember, seeks to uncover the congruence between our thoughts and the external world—the Coherence theory luxuriates in the weave and interplay of internal constancy.

Yet, this interlocking universe of ideas, with coherence as its judge and measure, comes with its own set of challenges. Critics contend that nestled within our networks of consistent beliefs, there might exist enclaves of false presuppositions, internally consistent yet disconnected or even contradictory to the rest of our beliefs. If coherence were the only criteria, these pockets of falsehood—internally coherent but ultimately untrue—might be labeled erroneously as truths.

Moreover, we encounter an issue of circularity: to say that a belief or statement is true because it's consistent with other beliefs presumes those other beliefs are themselves true. But on what basis is their truth determined? If it is their coherence with even more beliefs, we enter an infinite regress—an endless loop, a snake biting its own tail. Thus, the coherence theory's ideal—consistency within a mutually supportive network of beliefs—can at times veer disturbingly close to the edge of a relative realm where individual webs of belief, no matter how bizarre or fantastical, could each have their own truths if only they are internally coherent.

Yet while the Coherence theory undoubtedly provides fertile ground for philosophical debate, it also gives us an appreciable framework for navigating the tricky terrain of theoretical scientific concepts that may not yet—or may never—be fully subject to empirical verification. Theoretical physicists, for instance, wrestle with notions like dark matter and quantum entanglement, distinctly non-intuitive concepts which elude straightforward empirical testing, but whose place within theoretical frameworks accords them a type of truth value. They're considered truthful not in virtue of direct sensory correspondence, but through their coherence with a broader, well-established scientific theory.

Consider now that this theory stands not as an adversary to the Correspondence theory, but as an offering of alternative perspective—a reminder that sometimes, the truth is not demonstrated by a one-to-one correlation to the external world. It's a rallying cry against dogmatic absolutism, a reminder to remain humble in our search for knowledge, and to question both the reliability of our perceptions and the solidity of our internal principles.

The distinctive virtue of the coherence theory lies in the humility of its assumptions: it allows for the proposition that external reality might be a touch anarchic or even, in places, incomprehensible; that our capacity for understanding might not be the central axis upon which the universe turns. Instead of imposing an external carved reality, it prefers to arrange our pliable beliefs and thoughts into a harmonious, internally consistent structure.

From the intertwining beliefs of the Coherence theory, we take yet another leap: not towards a mirror reflection of reality or a harmonious mesh of ideas, but toward the consequential, the practical, the utilitarian. Let us now wade into the waters of the Pragmatic theory of truth – a doctrine that posits knowledge that serves us, that in practice works, is truthful.

At the heart of the Pragmatic theory of truth, we find not a desire for objective fact or internal consistency, but a preoccupation with the effects and outcomes of belief. To pragmatists, truth becomes tangible. It is a working process - a set of provisional truths evolving through practical application and the test of experience.

Let's pause for a moment and allow ourselves to envision truth not as a static point, but as the concerted action of a Swiss watch. Each hypothesis, resembling a cog in this watch, contributes to the overall functionality. If the watch exhibits congruity—if it keeps time perfectly—then this signifies each individual cog, each hypothesis, holds utility, thus truth.

The Pragmatic theory urges us to scrutinize our beliefs and test them against the crucible of lived experience—to assess them not, as the pragmatist William James puts it, for their relation to an "external reality," but rather for their practical benefits, for their workability: the fruits they bear in the lives of those who hold them. Herein, truth is no lofty intellectual or metaphysical abstraction, but rather it translates into a real influence on our lives.

To the pragmatist, the veracity of an idea is not measured by its precise alignment with reality or internal harmony but by its potency in prediction or problem-solving. A hypothesis that successfully predicts observed phenomena or aids in resolving a problem is endorsed by practical effect and henceforth considered true.

It is intriguing to imagine how this principle might extend to our everyday lives. Consider strategies we employ to navigate social situations, career choices, or lifestyle changes. Are they not subject to a form of pragmatic verification, their truthfulness determined not by their correspondence to external reality or internal consistency, but instead by the results they yield?

However, the Pragmatic theory of truth, despite its intuitive appeal, has found critics. Some argue that it sacrifices truth's purpose – representing reality – on the altar of mere usefulness. Take, for instance, the metaphor of a comforting illusion. If one was plagued by a sense of anxiety or fear, might they not invent a pacifying belief—say, that they are watched over by a guardian angel—to ease their stress? The pragmatic theory might deem this belief true if it was successful in its purposed function—easing anxiety. Critics, then, would expose this potential weakness, arguing that this approach risks alienating the concept of truth, unyoking it from its duty to reflect reality.

On the other hand, the aspect of utilitarianism intrinsic to the Pragmatic theory is by no means a wholesale dismissal of reality or the philosophical pursuit of truth. It is instead an acknowledgment that our understanding of the world, our truths, are inextricably yoked to experiences as living, thinking, and most importantly, acting beings.

Despite these considerations, one can't help but admire the Pragmatic theory's focus on inevitability and consequence, its attention to the fact that our beliefs inevitably meet with our experiences—that they do not, and cannot, exist in some insulated intellectual vacuum, but are instead always colliding with, bouncing against, and reverberating through our interactions with the world. In emphasizing the tangible effects of our ideas, the Pragmatic theory of truth roots itself firmly in the realm of lived experience and consequence.

Casting our eyes back over the paths we've traversed—the external alignment of the Correspondence theory, the internal harmonization of the Coherence theory, the practical consequences of the Pragmatic theory—we recognize we are navigating a terrain both diverse and complex. The pursuit of truth, it would appear, is not about establishing binary divisions of right and wrong but rather about exploring a web of relationships, probing the shadows, and seeking subtleties tucked away in the corners of our comprehension.

However, defining truth remains a daunting task, riddled with challenges and limitations. Our exploration of these theoretical representations casts light on some of these complexities, but teasing out the intricate fabric of truth provokes a few significant issues that deserve acknowledgment.

The variability of our human experience presents a significant challenge. Steeped in a diverse array of personal experiences and cultural backgrounds, we perceive reality differently. Every individual brings with them a unique lens through which they filter their interactions with the world, resulting in a kaleidoscope of diverse experiences even in identical environments. So, whose perspective would then offer the true representation of the event?

Language, that tool we so readily use to illustrate our understandings and bridge the gaps between our cognitive worlds, has its limitations. We speak in metaphors and similes, attempting to capture realities in nets of connotation and shared meanings, but we should not forget that language is just an approximation—a model, a map—not the reality it strives to depict. It sometimes lacks the precision needed to apprehend the exactness of a truth's nuance, diluting the potency of the idea it attempts to convey.

The pragmatist's lens brought into focus the ever-evolving, provisional nature of truth—a trait that coexists in uneasy tension with our intuitive desire for fixed, concrete reality. Indeed, another staggering challenge in defining truth is the fragility of our perceptions and understandings—they are not static. Our understanding of the world changes and adapts, propelled by scientific discovery and collective wisdom, continually reshaping our grasp on what we consider true.

Moreover, the concept of 'absolute truth,' an unwavering, incontestable fact, is prominently elusive. Untouched by human perceptions, interpretations, or cultural biases, such a claim stands firm and invincible in the face of contra evidence. However, does such a truth exist, insulated from the human experience? Capturing such truth would be akin to distilling the essence of the universe, untouched by the subjectivity of human interference—a task reaching into the realm of the meta-physical, and perhaps, the impossible.

26

The role of science in the pursuit of truth

Following in the wake of our exploration of truth, we find ourselves standing at the threshold of a not all too different domain. If pondering the nature of truth is akin to dissecting the anatomical structure of a wave, turning our focus to science could be compared to navigating the ocean from which the wave originates. Science presents us with an avenue to decode the mysteries of the universe while simultaneously underscoring our position within it.

Sciences' methodical and systematic approach is akin to an organized expedition, adhering to a prescribed route that is logically structured, meticulously planned, and persistently committed to objective inquiry. This expedition begins, incipiently, with an understanding that the world is intelligible. That is, the universe operates according to laws and patterns, and through systematic investigation and critical reasoning, we can gradually comprehend it.

Perching atop a centuries-long pyramid of knowledge—a commanding height built on the contributions of Galileo, Copernicus, Newton, and countless others—this perspective might, to us, seem self-evident. However, readily apparent as this may be to our modern mindset, the belief in an orderly, rational universe is by no means a given. Even today, not every culture shares this perspective, and there was a time when this was far from the prevalent worldview. Its origination—in the heart of the western world during the Age of Enlightenment—marked a colossal shift in humanity's approach to understanding reality.

An essential facet of science as a systematic approach to deciphering the natural world is its inherent iterative process. Scientists etch hypotheses on the pristine walls of ignorance, then launch investigations to disprove them. Thomas Kuhn, the philosopher of science, deemed these investigative endeavors 'normal science'. However, when a prevailing scientific paradigm encounters an anomaly it can't accommodate, there follows a period of 'extraordinary science'—a time of uncertainty and dissenting theories which eventually gives birth to a new paradigm reflecting an improved, more nuanced understanding of the universe.

While we often marvel at the monumental scientific discoveries and break-throughs, it's equally important to highlight the unheralded utility of failed experiments and discarded hypotheses. In their failure, they play a vital role, gradually chipping away at the vast monolith of the unknown, continuously shaping and refining our knowledge of the world. In this way, science is much like a master sculptor—meticulous, patient, and willing to learn from each incorrect strike of the chisel.

Underpinning the scientific process is a profound respect for evidence. Scientists painstakingly accumulate and analyze data, adhering to rigorous standards of statistical methods and replicability. They devise and conduct experiments that can yield falsifiable results, driven by a commitment to objectivity and truth. While human beings are innately inclined to interpret events and information in ways that reinforce existing beliefs, core to the scientific method is the principle that one must follow where the evidence leads, even if it overturns long-held theories or cherished beliefs.

Yet, it is crucial to remember that science, albeit a potent tool, is not the definitive arbiter of reality. It does not generate perfect, incontestable truths. Instead, it provides us with reliable, vetted, and continually evolving models of the world. These models serve as provisional truths, open to scrutiny and revision. In fact, the scientific method thrives on uncertainty. The acknowledgment of 'not knowing,' as we discussed earlier, is not an admission of defeat, but rather the fuel that propels the engine of scientific discovery.

In returning to our earlier metaphor and visualizing the scientific process as a grand expedition, we come to understand that the vessel employed for this endeavor—while sturdy and true—is by no means immutable. On the contrary, it is a ship in constant refurbishment, its design persistently revised and improved as discoveries are made, hypotheses refuted, and knowledge grows. This idea of self-correction lies at the heart of the scientific process.

This process, though often misunderstood, is not a linear progression leading from ignorance to an unequivocal truth. Instead, it is a ceaseless cycle of questioning, observing, hypothesizing, testing, analyzing, and refining—an often messy discourse punctuated by moments of divergence and convergence. It is much like a river—winding and twisting, sometimes peaceful, other times tumultuous, but always flowing forward, with both the river and those navigating it constantly adapting to the terrain to forge the optimal path.

As explored earlier, Charles Darwin offers an apt example of self-correction in action. Darwin initially hypothesized that evolution was a gradual process, with species changing slowly over time. Years later, this view was challenged by the theory of punctuated equilibrium, proposing that evolution is marked by long periods of stability punctuated by short episodes of rapid change. While this challenged Darwin's initial assertion, it did not negate his work--rather, it provided a new lens through which to view and interpret the dynamics of evolution. This is the beauty of science—it has the capacity to challenge, reshape, and refine its own understanding.

Undoubtedly, the scientific method educates us as participants and observers of this world that we inhabit. Yet, it does much more than that; it generates a narrative of humility in the face of nature's grandeur, a tale of constant self-scrutiny and open-mindedness. The ethic is simple: be curious, ask questions, seek evidence, and be willing to revise ideas when confronted with contrary evidence.

This constant quest for improvement is echoed by philosopher Karl Popper's concept of falsification, a cornerstone of scientific methodology. For an idea to qualify as scientific, he declared, there must be a conceivable empirical observation that could prove it false. When theories fail to meet their moment of falsification, they are not discarded outright, but rather reshaped, enhanced, their rough edges refined, their core framework fortified with the fresh steel of learning garnered from the confrontation with facts.

Far from a weakness, this potential for modification, this capacity for self-correction, is among the most enduring strengths of the scientific process. It spans across all disciplines, from the vast cosmos explored by astrophysicists to the tiny particles discovered by quantum physicists, from the secrets of DNA unravelled by geneticists to the complex ecosystem dynamics interpreted by ecologists.

In the realm of science, we must leave behind any notion that what we 'know' today is unassailable. We must be prepared to subordinate our desire for immediate understanding to the slow, careful, self-correcting exploration of truth. It's in this intersection of admission of the 'yet unknown' and the ceaseless pursuit for understanding that the brilliance of the self-correcting nature of science truly radiates. It's also essential to unabashedly confront the limitations of scientific knowledge.

Firstly, let us put forth this crucial reminder: The empirically observable universe, the object of study of the physical sciences, possesses a complexity almost beyond human comprehension. The sheer number of variables interacting in even the simplest of natural systems can make definitive conclusions elusive. From the subtle atomic dance playing out in the furthest galaxies to the intricate biological swirls in the smallest of earthly organisms, science grapples with phenomena of staggering intricacy. With each illuminating wave of discovery washing over our intellectual shore, so too comes the deepening recognition of just how much remains unknown. Said better, the more we learn, the more we realize how much there still is to learn.

Secondly, it behooves us to reflect upon the sobering truth that observation, the bedrock of empirical investigation, is inevitably tainted by interpretation, fashioned by the very nature of our human perception. Every lens through which we gaze, be it the humble magnifying glass or the Herculean Hubble Telescope, is invariably colored by the nature of our cognition, our existing knowledge, and our intrinsic biases. It's akin to trying to discern the true color of a landscape while peering through rose-tinted spectacles. Even the most accurate of apparatus reflects our human limitations and conveys a modulated image, not just of reality, but of our perception of reality.

Next, let's descend into the role of time and the evolving paradigms that come with its relentless march. For science always has, and always will, exist in a state of continual flux, shaped by the era it inhabits. Here's an experiment in time travel. Picture ourselves entrenched in the scientific milieu of the 19th century. Back then, the atom, indivisible by definition, was considered the smallest unit of matter. Fast-forward to the 21st century, and what we know of the atom has been utterly transformed—the 'indivisible' has been divided, and then divided again! Thus, today's truths can become tomorrow's quaint misconceptions, a testament not to science's instability, but rather to its evolution in the face of new knowledge. Science's very foundation is the understanding that today's certainty may not withstand tomorrow's scrutiny.

David Bohm, a physicist of substantial renown, emphasized the need for a science attuned to flux rather than certainty, one that remains open to intrinsic unpredictability, much like the quantum realm he so ardently explored. This notion of "unfolding" knowledge propounds that facts do not exist in isolation, but form a part of an ever-evolving understanding of reality. In this worldview, the quest for knowledge is a journey without a finite destination, akin to a novel that continues to write itself, the plot twists shaped by the characters we inevitably bump into (or discover) along the way.

When we place science upon this panoramic canvas, we move beyond a compartmentalized understanding—a force fitting of puzzle pieces into an existing frame—and we begin dancing to the symphony of the cosmos, where the notes and the music itself are part of a wider, continuously evolving composition. And what a liberating and humbly ground-shaking, worldview-shattering composition it is!

We must adopt the words of Richard Feynman, a true servant of curiosity, who eloquently stated, "I would rather have questions that can't be answered than answers that can't be questioned."

27

The role of emotions and intuition in ascertaining truth

Having grappled with the far reaches of intellectual knowledge and the intriguing, occasionally confounding, world of scientific understanding, it is time for us to turn our gaze inwards, towards our own subjective emotional and intuitive experiences.

Through the kaleidoscope of life, emotions and intuition, often twins in their tandem working, emerge with an undeniable potency. They wield the power to shape our worldviews, determine our actions, and ultimately, construct our reality. Beneath the veneer of every decision, every leap and recess, every emotional and intuitive experience, lies a deeper truth—the truth about who we are and how we navigate the universe unfolding around us.

Emotions, those colorful dabs of inner vitality, paint our lives with shades unparalleled in their diversity. They have the power to plunge us into the melancholy blues of sorrow, and in a fleeting instant, propel us to the radiant yellows of joy. Their brilliance is matched only by their ability to shape not just our moments, but our identities and even our worldview. Take love, for instance, an emotion so profound it has spawned entire movements,

179

started and ended wars, and unknowingly predicted patterns of migration. It wields the power to make us move mountains—both metaphorical and real. Emotional experiences are not merely internal, subjective phenomena. They ripple out, extending their influence to the world around us, refracting through the prism of our interactions and relationships.

Just as emotions offer us a unique lens to view and interpret the world, our intuition bestows upon us the uncanny ability to 'know' or 'feel' things instinctively. Circling the mystery of intuition feels akin to walking into a lavish magic show—the tricks and illusions mystify, the guessing games bewitch, but the 'how' of it all remains shrouded in obscurity. Intuition is the murmur in the background, the unseen hand behind the curtain of our conscious reasoning, guiding and shaping our decisions with a subtlety that barely flits across our conscious awareness.

We have all experienced that uncanny hunch, the 'gut feeling' that stubbornly nudges us towards a particular direction, seemingly devoid of rational basis. It's that sensation that something is amiss, even when an objective appraisal of the situation suggests all is well. It's the inexplicable pull towards a chance encounter or an opportunity that, against all odds, turns out to be a game-changer. Our intuitive experiences are the subtle murmurs, the whispers in the wind that guide our sail across the vast seas of existence.

Yet, despite the near-ubiquity and overwhelming influence of emotions and intuition, we often downplay their role when we talk about truth. Derived as they are from the deeply subjective, the personalized, and the non-rational aspects of our cognition—we may question the legitimacy of the truths they purport. We teeter on the precipice of a profound paradox—the duality of rationality, honed by science and logic on the one hand, and emotions and intuition, deeply rooted in our subjective experiences on the other.

Launching from the exploration of emotions and intuition, we find ourselves drawn towards empathy—a facet of our emotional competence that plays a crucial role in our perception of truth. Empathy not only enables us to understand and share another's emotional state but also opens a channel to appreciate and perceive their reality—their truth. Building bridges of emotional resonance, empathy allows us to shift from the solitary island of selfhood to shared experiential geography.

Two distinct, yet interwoven strands, weave the intricate web of empathy. Cognitive empathy, often called perspective-taking, allows us to comprehend the thoughts and emotions of others. We do not merely 'feel for' them, but 'feel with' them. Emotional empathy, on the other hand, moves beyond the realm of understanding into the space of shared feeling, where another's pain becomes our pain, their joy ours.

Imagine yourself sitting across from a friend, engrossed in their recounting of a recent heartbreak. As their voice trembles and eyes well up, you find a lump forming in your throat, a heaviness weighing your heart—symptoms most accurately diagnosed as empathy. You've walked a mile in their shoes, and their heartbreak has become a shared experience. This empathy allows you to extract a deeper truth from their story—a truth that a mere objective assessment could not reveal. You've perceived the truth not merely through their words, but through interpreting the ebb and flow of their emotions, their quivering voice, and teary eyes.

In a world increasingly characterized by diversity and heterogeneity, empathy takes center stage as a tool for understanding other perspectives—their experiences, their emotions, and their truths. Empathy breaks down barriers, exposing us to the richness and complexity of human experience, transforming our understanding of truth from a stark, monochromatic monoculture into a vibrant multicultural mosaic.

Yet the power of empathy extends beyond cultivating individual connections. It reaches its full potential when it acts as an agent for collective understanding. Empathy stirs the cauldron of social discourse, thaws the icy divide between conflicting viewpoints, and nudges society towards a more nuanced understanding of the collective truth. It is empathy that allows the stories of marginalized communities to be heard, their struggle recognized, and their reality understood.

Take, for instance, the repercussions of stories from the #MeToo movement. They have opened our eyes, through empathetic understanding, to the disquieting reality faced by countless women around the world. The truths revealed through shared personal narratives, powered by empathy, have forced a global reckoning—making us question societal norms and seek reforms, driven by the shared truth of these experiences.

Empathy also plays a critical role in situations of conflict resolution. Whether in personal relations or global diplomacy, empathy allows us to perceive the truth of the 'other'. It enables us to discern the varying shades of truth that color human conflict, helping us appreciate the complex multidimensionality of truth. The acceptance of these various realities can pave the way for amicable resolutions that acknowledge and respect each party's truth.

While empathy is a potent tool for understanding others, it is not without its limitations. Empathy can sometimes lead to distress if the emotional burden becomes too heavy, or result in 'empathetic bias', where we may understand and empathize with those who are similar to or close to us, but struggle to extend this understanding to those who are different. It is important to acknowledge these potential pitfalls, even as we recognize empathy's immense strength in perceiving truth.

We now turn the page to an equally influential determinant of our grasp of reality - personal experiences and gut feelings. These powerful forces serve to write the narrative of what we accept as truth, based on experiential learning and deep-seated instincts.

Across history, the gut often has been referred to as a 'second brain', a reservoir of guidance, grounded in instinct, emotion, and stored experience. It is a dialect spoken without language – a product of intuition whispering advice, albeit through the language of feelings. It's the churning in your stomach, the Goosebumps on your arm, or that nagging feeling that something is 'off.' Familiar to everyone, such common phenomena become our personal compass, navigating us through the seas of uncertainty and ever-evolving truths.

Have you ever been faced with a decision that on paper seemed perfect, but something inexplicable stirred within you, a deep-rooted feeling, advising caution? This is the visceral voice of your gut, your intuition, sending signals from the depth of your subconscious mind, based on your past experiences, patterns recognized, learning, and inherent survival instinct. At times, your conscious-rational mind may wrestle with these flags, often dismissing them as irrational, but the fascinating reality is, these gut feelings can reveal a layer of truth that mere logical reasoning may overlook.

Our personal experiences, too, are significant architects of our perceived truth. By shaping our perspectives, these experiences create a framework through which we navigate our world, interpret events, and formulate our truths. Every experience acts as a stroke of the brush, gradually painting the canvas of our worldview. They become our reference points, our anchoring docks in the vast, tempestuous sea of life, offering interpretive guidance as we encounter new circumstances.

Think of a traumatic experience from your past. When a similar scenario presents itself in the future, the 'truth' of the potential threat derived from your past experience sets off alarm bells. This experiential learning emerges from the subconscious and guides your reactions. While the solidity of the current threat might be arguable, your truth, borne out from past experience, stands undeniable.

However, the same tapestry of experiences also serves to caution us against the potential drawbacks of relying too heavily on personal perceptions and gut instincts. It can create a 'reality tunnel' - a subconscious type of tunnel vision whereby we interpret every situation through the lens of our past experiences. Our 'gut' might convince us, for example, never to trust again after a heartbreak, or that success is forbidden territory after repeated failures.

Do these gut feelings and experiences, then, present the undiluted truth? No. They are whispers from the past and present, guiding us based on what we've seen, heard, felt, and learned.

Gut feelings and personal experiences, though valuable, can tend towards over-simplification and quick judgment, disregarding the complexity and multi-faceted nature of truth. The familiar grooves created by past experiences may not accurately fit the fresh mold of current circumstances. Also, our guts can be flawed; susceptible to the noise of fear, anxiety, desire, and other emotional influences that may cloud instinctual signals.

At this crossroads, an equilibrium must be sought, a balance achieved between the rational and the emotional, the objective and the subjective. This pivotal interaction of the cognitive and affective domains leads us to an understanding that is closer to the truth, one that considers the complexity and diversity of human experiences, rather than tries to fit them into packed boxes.

When guided singularly by logic, we run the risk of suppressing the authentic, valuable insights that our emotions and feelings offer. Conversely, if we navigate solely by the compass of our emotions or experiences, we may tumble into the abyss of irrationality. This brings forth an intriguing question: How do we maneuver these intertwined pathways of thought and feeling?

A balanced approach requires us to integrate – to allow space for both stalwart logical analysis and that quiet instinctual voice. It involves embracing emotional intelligence along with rational logic, to generate a nuanced understanding of reality. Imagine emotional intelligence as a soft light illuminating the contours and crevices of a path that our logical flashlight may disregard in its quest for focus and precision.

With this in balance, we become skilled at deciphering our emotions, values, and experiences, mapping them accurately, while concurrently, unwavering in our objective pursuit of the rational. This amalgam of emotional intelligence and rational thought ensures we embrace our human nature – intuitive, emotional, and experiential – and logically evaluate and comprehend experiences.

An emotionally intelligent individual endeavors to understand others and their motivations, seeks commonalities despite differences, and reads the subtle emotional cues often overlooked when an analytical approach dominates. They may possess insights tucked away from the glaring light of traditional logic.

However, being emotionally intelligent doesn't mean abandoning the rigor of rational thought. It is the process of considering emotions without being dominated by them, acknowledging instinctual murmurs but affirming them with intelligent reflection. Similar to a chess player, who, in every move, accounts for both the emotional desire to win and the logical strategy that must guide the pursuit of that win.

Emotional intelligence and rationality are not at loggerheads. Abstract rational thought unaided by the context of emotional significance may be like a ship sailing blind. In contrast, emotions without the anchor of logical reasoning might drift astray in a tornado. By integrating emotions and reasoning, we invite a deeper truth - one more reflective of the dynamic human experience.

This harmonious fusion of feeling and thinking, the intellect, and the heart, enables us to tread the path towards truth with a balanced gait – responsive to our personal experiences and intuitive signals, yet not captive to them. It is through this striking balance, embracing vulnerability, while being resilient in our inquiry, that we cultivate intellectual humility. It allows us to murmur, with a comforting certainty, "I don't know."

Turning our attention from the artist, culture, now let's consider the varying canvases where they paint their masterpieces – the context. The influence of the backdrop, the setting, the scene – they all contribute, in large strokes, to the picture that finally emerges as truth. Truth in its essence has a slippery nature; it morphs and melds, shapeshifts and shimmers based on where and when it is held up to the light.

Let's first contemplate time's serpentine trail on the evolution of truth. We all share the common knowledge that Earth is indeed, not the center of our solar system, but a planet orbiting a star in a corner of a vast universe. Yet, there was a time when this was not so. The thought of a moving, non-central Earth appearing as a disruptive claim, one against the 'truth' as it was perceived, is a testament to how normative context and time can mold understanding.

Context also moves with us spatially, shaping our perceptions based on immediate surroundings. It isn't uncommon for the setting to induce clarity or generate fog that clouds our perspectives. For instance, one's accurate reading of a person's character might be disturbed by a discomforting, unfamiliar environment. We might perceive someone to be rude or aloof when we first meet them at a crowded party but realize they were just overwhelmed when we encounter them later in a more intimate setting.

Context also wields its power through societal norms and institutional frameworks that we live within. From a macroscopic view, these structures can classify certain behaviors as unlawful or immoral, shaping the collective truth about social propriety. Conversely, from a microscopic lens, even within these large structures, sub-contexts arise that nudge our perceptions. Office politics, educational settings, or neighborhood dynamics – each of these mini-contexts come with their rules, influencing how individuals perceive and respond to situations.

Not only are these contexts subjective, governed by societal norms, but they can also be provoked by personal experiences—these individualistic contexts birthed from past events and relationships cast a different light on truth. An individual who had been bitten by a dog in childhood may carry a deep-seated fear of dogs, cultivating their truth around these animals as dangerous, which contrasts with the experiences of a person who grew up with dogs as family pets.

Another shade of contextual coloring arises from the power dynamics at play. These dynamics, often underpinned by social inequality or disparity, can introduce a bias that tints the narrative of truth. Efforts to preserve power can lead to a distorted representation of facts or experiences, presenting them in a manner that fortifies the existing structure. For instance, history, often written by winners, can bear a favorable tilt towards the powerful, subtly casting the vanquished as deserving of their fate.

In even subtler notes, the nuances of language and communication contextualize our understanding of truth. We choose words, style, tone, and rhythm not just based on what we wish to convey, but also considering the context in which a message is received. The receiver's interpretation then weaves another layer of context, factoring individual understanding and emotional states.

Yet, even in this complex weave of context, one must strive for lucidity to reach towards an authentic comprehension of truth. Recognizing that context has its fingerprints on every perception empowers us to dissect its influence, allowing for a more multifaceted and balanced perspective in truth-seeking. However, since it may not be within our reach to entirely eliminate the context's sway, we ought to debate its validity and question its implications.

It's here we find ourselves at an intersection where the plurality of perceptions spins, and where a congress of conflicting truths congregates. What then is the forward path? How can divergence converge into a shared common ground? It lies forged in empathy, respect, and a commitment to dialogue.

The proposition of a shared common ground doesn't necessarily imply merging all perspectives into a single, unanimous viewpoint. However, it does involve recognizing and validating these different viewpoints, fostering a culture that cherishes diversity and encourages dialogue. The pursuit of this common ground sways between the nuances of empathy and the call for reason.

Empathy, the capacity to understand or feel what another person is experiencing, allows us to temporarily step into another's shoes. Training our empathetic muscle to flex within the realm of intellectual discourse means providing a benevolent ear, striving to comprehend not just the 'why' but the 'how' of differing perspectives. Like an explorer tracing back a river to its source, the empathetic interlocutor aims to understand the genesis of contrasting viewpoints, traveling upstream to the point where difference diverged.

It's through empathy that we accommodate the other's contextual truth within our cognitive horizon, thereby paving the way for acknowledgement. Acknowledgement, in this case, does not necessarily mean an agreement or convergence of truths, but a respectful recognition of the legitimacy of the other's perspective. It is about gracing their viewpoint with sensitivity and respectful validation, even when it sits at odds with ours.

Yet, empathy alone runs the risk of perpetuating inaccuracies under the guise of equality. Hence, the tandem partner in this dance is balanced dialogue, which ensures substantiated truths take precedence over misinformed or biased perspectives. A respectful dialogue is one where we honor the other's viewpoint but also challenge and ask for their evidence and reasoning. Yielding ground to a differing perspective is only as essential as confirming the authenticity of the evidence on which that view anchors.

This brings us to the heart of any productive dialogue – the willingness of all parties to listen, learn, and grow. This manifests in the mutual commitment towards revising one's views in the light of compelling evidence and arguments. However, this asks for stripping one's beliefs of egotistical attachment and admitting, when necessary, ignorance, or better yet, error. This challenging act of cognitive humility forms the bedrock of a progressive dialogue and is central to the evolution of knowledge and understanding.

In this respect, individuals and societies can borrow a leaf from the pages of science. The scientific world thrives on the principle of falsifiability. It's a principle that foregrounds the perpetual provisional nature of knowledge and encourages intellectual humility. As theories compete, they're subjected to rigorous experiments to validate their predictive power. Empirical evidence counts more than elegant philosophy.

Along these lines, we can foster a shared knowledge-arena. Divergent views and conflicting truths are welcomed, provided they are open to the rigorous examination of empirical evidence, logical consistency, and impartial reasoning. A commitment to follow the evidence, no matter where it leads, irrespective of cherished beliefs or notions, is integral to erecting the scaffolding of this arena.

Deliberate discourse is not about stubborn retreat into ideological fortresses. Instead, an inclusive exchange of ideas offers a fertile playground where ignorance is not suppressed but acknowledged, contested truths are not discarded but examined, and intellectual humility is not weakness but courageous inquiry. It's this shared pursuit of enlightenment that celebrates the diversity of experiences while moving towards a collective understanding of 'truth'.

Therefore, seeking common ground may not result in a homogenized, unified truth, but it will facilitate a richer, more nuanced understanding of diverse realities. It calls for replacing confrontation with conversation, disorder with dialogue, and battle with empathy, birthing a symphony that celebrates the uniqueness of differences and the harmony of convergence.

28

The benefits and potential dangers of provisional truths

In the grand scheme of evolving human knowledge and understanding, we find ourselves standing on the slippery ground of provisional truths. These are truths susceptible to change, revision, and metamorphosis under the flux of newfound data, observations, alternative hypotheses, and the test of time. Encouraging open-mindedness and adaptability, thus, becomes an essential strategy in dealing with this ever-modifiable nature of truth.

The concept of open-mindedness forms the cornerstone of intellectual growth. To be open-minded entails recognizing the fluidity of our beliefs and truths, and being receptive to modifications in light of incisive arguments, powerful encounters, or novel information. It confronts us with the challenging endeavour of holding our convictions lightly, ready to revise or let them go if they fail to marry up to the standards of evidence or coherent reasoning.

Moreover, open-mindedness invites the possibility of 'not-knowing,' a state of acknowledging that there are things yet unknown to us, aspects of our knowledge incomplete or flawed. It's this perpetual curiosity and unwillingness to settle in the comfort of certainty that fuels our journey towards enlightenment. Open-mindedness, thus, becomes a silent admission of our inability to completely comprehend a complex, multi-dimensional universe.

Yet, the path to open-mindedness is not without its obstacles. We are creatures of habit, favoring order and predictability above unexpected detours and disruptions. Our minds have evolved to succumb to the seductive pull of cognitive biases that breed the illusion of certainty. Battling these deep-seated tendencies requires a degree of self-awareness and a determination to step out of comfort zones filled with preconceived assumptions and biases.

The story doesn't end with fostering open-mindedness as adaptability seamlessly connects to it, forming the yin to its yang. Adaptability refers to the ability to adjust to new conditions, incorporate new strategies, and shift one's outlook in response to the undulating currents of information and evidence that mold the riverbed of truth. It includes not simply accepting, but embracing changes as part of the unfolding tapestry of knowledge.

Adaptability promotes the readiness not only to change our minds but our actions, reactions and strategies accordingly. It fuels our ability not merely to survive but to thrive amidst the ever-fluctuating walkways of provisional truths. Absence of adaptability can lead to cognitive rigidity, where outdated beliefs and unproductive strategies are clung to, even in the face of compelling evidence suggesting a revision. In contrast, an adaptable mind is like clay, firm yet malleable, retaining structure yet open to reshaping as it learns and grows.

Coupling open-mindedness and adaptability sheds light on a significant aspect of dealing with provisional truths - the capacity to entertain a thought without adopting it immediately. This mental exercise allows us to introspectively hold, examine, and evaluate perspectives that conflict with our current understanding, without letting our prejudices color our discernment.

However, it's prudent to mention that adaptability and open-mindedness are not to be confused with susceptibility. An open, adaptable mind is not an empty vessel ready to be filled with every fringe idea or baseless hypothesis. It maintains a discerning filter, a riposte against misinformation, grounded in rigorous scientific method, logical consistency and empiricism.

In the process of encouraging open-mindedness and adaptability in response to provisional truths, we find a precipice looming on the horizon: the risk of moral relativism and a deficiency of conviction. Moral relativism, a perspective contending the absence of universal moral truths, epitomizes a stretch of open-mindedness teetering on being overplayed—turning from a boon to a potential liability.

A moral relativist's world is one that declines to recognize simplified distinctions between right and wrong, good and bad. The lack of objectivity concerning morality in such a viewpoint can, in turn, lead to a floundering of ideals and principles. If every moral belief becomes simply a reflection of a person's individual perspective or cultural group, then finding common ethical ground to adjudicate disputes or conflicts carries the risk of becoming an elusive endeavor. By espousing such a perspective, we broadly open ourselves to the ethical tectonics of shifting societal trends, making moral compasses susceptible to the winds of cultural change.

This moral uncertainty opens a Pandora's box of questions: Can any behavior be reprehensibly labeled 'wrong' or 'unethical' if it aligns with the perpetrator's ethical system or belief? Can justice be served in a world borrowing from cultural relativism, where heinous acts might be justified under the banner of tradition or custom? These questions serve to bring into focus the dangerous precipice upon which moral relativism teeters.

What plays as a concomitant to moral relativism is the lack of conviction—an idea not foreign to the landscape of open-mindedness and adaptability. It's an inherent risk accompanying the pursuit of changing truths—when we internalize the fluidity of truth, we may also inadvertently make fluid our conviction in our values and beliefs. As a result, conviction threatens to lose its strength, becoming paper-thin under the strain of incessant alteration.

However, the lack of conviction should not be mistaken as a sign of weakness or indecisiveness. Instead, it plays out as a side-effect of a mind constantly fluxing and adapting to new sets of information and experiences. Unlike blind adherence to static beliefs, this lack of unchanging conviction allows a person to change, grow, and evolve. While this might appear unsettling, it is this very process that stretches the horizons of knowledge and understanding.

Still, having a lack of conviction running unchecked could lead one to waver at the sight of every new perspective, to be swayed by every wave in the ocean of opinions. We could find ourselves adrift, anchorless in a sea of fast-moving trends and ephemeral truths, risking our ability to stand firm when the situation warrants it.

Being tolerant and accepting of diverse perspectives doesn't mean we need to lose our grounding or principles. While our understanding of truth is provisional and malleable, our formed perspectives based on careful thought, thorough research, and our personal experiences and values do not lose their relevance. Instead, they adapt and evolve, maintaining their core integrity while marginal beliefs are pruned, and new insights are incorporated. This process both guards against an uncritical acceptance of every newly presented truth and gives us a flexible structure on which to hang our evolving understanding.

In the end, it's essential to strike a balance—a balance that champions the virtues of open-mindedness, adaptability and humility paired with a commitment to keen discernment, deep reflection, and thoughtful judgment. The quest for truth, then, becomes a dynamic dance of tension and resolution, a dynamic balance of core convictions and intellectual adaptability—a dance that celebrates the spirit of intellectual humility amidst the changing landscapes of perceived truths.

In holding the tension of paradox between unyielding conviction and limitless adaptability, we encounter the potential for immeasurable growth and progress ignited by provisional truths. If the acceptance of moral relativism and a lack of conviction implies the prospect of danger, could the converse not carry the promise of intellectual evolution and societal development?

By treating truth as provisional, we essentially invoke the spirit of continuous learning. This invites us to humbly accept that today's hard-won knowledge might be tomorrow's obsolete insight, and opens the door to a world of endless learning. Such a posture of intellectual humility, where the bond to absolute certainty is loosened, becomes not a liability, but an asset. By imbuing our understating of truth with the capacity for change, we position ourselves for ongoing growth and constant refinement of understanding.

Progress, both personal and societal, is stood on the stepping stones of provisional truths. It has been the hunger to question, to doubt, and to contravene our assumptions that has defined humanity's growth from the earliest form of fire starters to the latest in quantum physics. The cultivation of wonder and curiosity, the intellectual humility to accept that we do not hold the ultimate answer, yields a nursery for innovation. Take for example, the momentous shift in perspective when humankind, once certain of an earth-centric universe, opened their minds to the heliocentric model. Provisional truths encouraged growth and progression in our knowledge, moving us from the comfort of certainty to the frontiers of uncertainty.

The advent of science is a poignant example of how the adoption of provisional truths could bring about radical change. Before the scientific revolution, 'truth' was often dictated by religious institutional authority or philosophical conjecture. However, the birth of the scientific method—grounded in observation, hypothesis, experiment, and reconsideration—transformed the pursuit of truth entirely. Our understanding transitioned from being sealed to open-ended, conditioned to accumulate, substantiate, and even contradict what was previously held as 'truth'. This embracement of provisional truths initiated an explosion of transformative discoveries, from Newton's laws to Einstein's Theory of Relativity, each breaking and then reconstructing humanity's understanding of reality.

Recognizing the provisional nature of 'truth' is akin to learning how to navigate within a shifting maze. It is to acknowledge that the map is not the territory. It necessitates us to develop the flexibility and adaptability to recalibrate our route as the terrain of knowledge morphs. Our beliefs, ideas, even the principles we live by, become evolving entities—expanding, contracting, and morphing in response to the gales and currents of ongoing learning.

Somewhat paradoxically, this seeming dance with uncertainty is also key in fostering resilience. Imagine, if you will, a willow tree standing tall amidst strong winds. Rather than resisting the gusts, the willow bends, its branches yielding but not breaking. Similarly, our intellect, when embracing the concept of provisional truths, becomes like the willow, strong yet flexible, anchored yet adaptable—a characteristic crucial in this volatile, ambiguous, complex world we currently inhabit.

In essence, accepting truth as provisional equips us with the intellectual humility to mitigate cognitive biases, fallacies, and traps detailed in previous chapters. The understanding of the fallibility of our own cognitive faculties is the impetus for the necessity to remain open to evidence that contradicts our reasoning, to question our assumed truths, and actively seek differing perspectives. To continue the growth and progress through provisional truth, we must encourage robust dialogue, diverse perspectives, and ensure that respect for evidence and rationality is central to our quest for truth.

The courage to dwell in uncertainty, to embrace the changeability of 'truth', becomes an intellectual vanguard, allowing us not only to survive but to thrive amidst change. It becomes an invitation to marvel at the intricate dance between conviction and adjustability—to capture the spirit of intellectual humility amidst the ever-fluctuating shape of an evolving universe. In the end, as we thread this complex labyrinth, perhaps we may even find that the wisdom lies not in the reaching of the end, but in the richness of the journey itself.

29

How Intellectual Humility Spurs Growth and Progress

We have arrived at a point where intellectual humility stands as an elemental pillar, the Archimedean point, if you will. It balances our acceptance of provisional truths and our pursuit of knowledge amidst an ever-evolving landscape of understanding. Abandoning the safety of rigid certainty for the fluid motion of intellectual growth, we ignite the fire for continual learning, questioning, and dialogue. This mental shift, this openness, is the essence of intellectual humility—a concept we now delve deeper into.

Intellectual humility, often misconstrued as a sign of softer convictions, especially in a society that celebration relentless assertion, is a decidedly fortifying virtue in its own right. Nursing a willingness to revise one's beliefs in the light of new information, it underpins the perpetual drive toward truth. For truth, as we have explored, is not a static monument, but a dynamic, living tapestry—ever-evolving as we constantly unravel realities and understandings of our intricate universe.

If we liken our quest for truth to navigating a dynamic, puzzling, and ever-changing terrain, intellectual humility is the compass guiding us through the shadows of ignorance towards the glimmers of understanding. It asks us not to plant ourselves in the fortress of dogma, but to step into the open arena of learning. It encourages us not to armor ourselves in known ideas, but to courageously unshutter ourselves in the face of the unknown. By doing so, we present ourselves the opportunity for growth, evolution, error, and correction—a cocktail of elements integral to the pursuit of truth.

Herein lies the paradoxical power of intellectual humility, stirring within the gentle vulnerability of admitting our limitations, and within the audacious strength of changing our convictions. By understanding that our grasp on the truth is tentative and subject to revision, we echo the wisdom of Socrates—who recognized his knowledge as infinitesimal against the grand backdrop of the unknown. Embodying this enlightenment necessitates the shedding of hubris and the adoption of a mindset that says, "I am willing to learn, to change, and to adapt."

Fundamentally, intellectual humility is not the admission of weak intellect but the acceptance of our cognitive faculties' limitations, as explored throughout this text. It doesn't stand as a reflective failure of our intelligence, but it subtly highlights the resilience and adaptability of our learning, the capacity to endure the ebb and flow of evolving truths. The light of intellectual humility illuminates the murky waters of fallacies and biases, reminding us of the accuracy of our perception and the fallibility of our cognition.

Intellectual humility, thus, remaps the pursuit of truth. It redefines progress not as a rugged, triumphant march towards a predetermined destination, but a thoughtful dance—a waltz, perhaps—between knowledge and discovery, conviction and curiosity, understanding and questioning. It fosters a climate where dialogue, diversity of thought, and cross-pollination of ideas can flourish—echoing the essence of intellectual growth.

If intellectual humility is the compass guiding us through the terrain of truth, then withholding judgment and embracing doubt are the very act of following that compass, not deviating toward safe yet misleading paths. The decision to refrain from immediate judgment and instead, entertain the whispers of doubt is in itself, an act underscoring the strength of intellectual humility in our pursuit of truth.

Withholding judgement isn't an act of passivity or inability to form an opinion. Rather, it is a thoughtful and conscious pause, a momentary suspension of our verdicts to allow for a wider universe of understanding to permeate our intellectual filters. It is about giving the stage to information that can counter our established beliefs, and daring to entertain them.

In a social ecosystem that thrives on speed, efficiency, and swift verdicts, withholding judgment can feel counterintuitive, perhaps even an impediment. But let's imagine, for a moment, our cognitive evolution as a grand symphony. Each note representing a nugget of truth, every chord an accepted belief, each rest a pause opening the possibility of sound. What would happen if we began to play all the notes simultaneously, without any rests, in our eager hurry? The music wouldn't be harmonious; it would become a cacophony. Withholding judgment, in the symphony of our cognition, then, is these intentional, valuable, rests—an opportunity for the music to breathe, to uncover hidden melodies, and to make sense of the evolving harmony.

Embracing doubt, on the other hand, is the yin to the yang of withholding judgment. Where withholding judgment requires courage, embracing doubt involves vulnerability. To invite doubt is to crack open the door of our intellectual fortress and allow the winds of contrasting perspectives to freely pass through. It makes us aware of the scope of what we don't know, sparking curiosity and sprouting the seeds of intellectual growth.

In a society that often regards doubt as a sign of weakness, embracing it can be a daunting experience. However, the beauty of doubt lies in its uncanny ability to challenge the status quo, to question the validity of accepted truths, and to provide the friction necessary for the flame of new understanding to ignite. Just as the finest swords are forged in the most intense flames, our most insightful revelations are born from the heat of our doubts.

Embracing doubt also arrests our familiar descent into hasty conclusions, fueled by cognitive biases. It transforms our relationship with uncertainty from one of apprehension to understanding. In opening the gates of our cognition to doubt, we invite truth, conceived out of dialogue with contrasting perspectives, to grace our intellectual domain.

Considering the significant role played by withholding judgment and embracing doubt in our cognitive evolution, we yet remain driven by the primal curiosity inherent to our species. The intellectual humility, achieved by mastering these arts, sets the stage for a culture of curiosity, learning, and collaboration.

The fostering of such an intellectual culture has profound societal implications. It effectively mushrooms into knowledge-societies that represent the finest manifestation of human ambition to seek, understand, and share wisdom. These societies are treasure troves of intellectual dynamism and human progress and lean heavily on three pillars: curiosity, learning, and collaboration.

Curiosity, in this context, is the spark. It's the primeval human instinct that provoked the first hominid to pick up a stone tool, induced Newton to question the fall of an apple, and ignited the desire in Neil Armstrong to take that historic leap on the moon. Curiosity expands the horizons of our understanding, pushing us into unchartered neural territories and paving the way for new knowledge.

Within communities that cherish intellectual humility, curiosity assumes a heightened stature. It's not just a mere personal instinct but a collective pursuit, a shared endeavor. It incites us to question what we know and emboldens us to admit what we don't. Curiosity navigates us through the dense fog of ignorance by a compass calibrated by the true north of 'I don't know.'

However, curiosity without an accommodating infrastructure is like a unignited matchstick; it holds potential yet lacks the flame. Learning is the reaction that illuminates the darkness with the flame of knowledge. It is the transformative process that transmutes raw curiosity into refined wisdom. It fosters the accumulation, synthesis, and evolution of knowledge; it urges us to confront the unknown, grapple with it, and integrate it into our intellectual repertoire.

Learning, catalyzed by curiosity and supercharged in a humble mind, illuminates the path to truth but is not a solitary endeavor. It is a dialogue, a transaction, a spirited exchange between the self and the world. Such reciprocity breathes life into the third pillar of knowledge societies – collaboration.

Collaboration is the visible hand that threads isolated pockets of knowledge into a cohesive understanding. It is the silent consensus among learners to pool their intellectual resources and attack problems of grand scale with shared might. Collaboration is the melting pot of varied intellectual traditions, different perspectives, and unique thinking styles that yield robust solutions, novel insights, and innovative ideas.

In an environment where curiosity kickstarts intellectual quests, learning chips away at ignorance, and collaboration rounds up the knowledge forces, intellectual humility becomes the orchestrator of this grand symphony. It injects the rhythm of modesty into the aggressive melody of curiosity, maintains a steady beat of doubt to the volatile harmony of learning, and amplifies the subtle undertones of diversity in the powerful chorus of collaboration.

Thus, societies that craft a culture centered around curiosity, learning, and collaboration, with intellectual humility as the scaffolding, contribute profoundly to the relentless human pursuit of truth. These communities demonstrate the possible – of what we can achieve collectively when we momentarily silence the inflated 'I know' to make way for the more empowering and enlightening 'I don't know.'

V

Harnessing AI to Overcome Cognitive Barriers and Propel Humanity Forward

30

The rise of AI

As we have journeyed together through the landscape of human intelligence—a terrain as fascinating as it is fragile—we have come to see the startling paradoxes that govern our cognition. Capable of producing breathtaking feats of innovation and poetic insight, our minds can also ensnare us in a tangled web of biases, fallacies, and other cognitive hiccups. The path we have traced so far has underscored one profound truth: the richness of human thought is inseparable from its pitfalls.

In this tumultuous world where knowledge seems both tantalizingly near and frustratingly elusive, we now turn our gaze towards a potential ally in our quest for self-improvement. Artificial intelligence (AI), once confined to the realm of science fiction, is increasingly changing the way we live, work, and think. As these technologies infiltrate every aspect of our day-to-day lives and continue their unrelenting march towards an ever deeper understanding of our world, their impact on our cognitive ecosystems becomes impossible to ignore.

This fifth part of our exploration will delve into the power and potential held within AI—an array of technological marvels that may well hold the key to suppressing cognitive hurdles and championing intellectual humility in ways previously unattainable. To appreciate this possibility fully, we must first acquaint ourselves with AI's history—those serendipitous accidents, brilliant insights, and persistent efforts that have brought us here today.

From humble beginnings in Turing machines to impressive advancements in machine learning brought about by neural networks and deep learning algorithms, we shall trace the evolution of AI back through time and space. United by a common thread of curiosity and purposefulness, this narrative unfolds against a backdrop of scientific progress marked by breakthrough after breakthrough.

Yet what lies at the heart of this story is not merely a journey through time, but an odyssey towards the future—one where humanity may harness AI's incredible power to counteract the very biases and fallacies we have identified throughout this book. Can artificial intelligence help us break free from the shackles of our own cognitive limitations? How might AI shape the way we seek truth, both as individuals and collectively, nurturing our capacity for intellectual humility even as it expands our horizons?

Together, we will examine case studies in which AI has empowered scientific inquiry, aided in collaboration amongst diverse perspectives, and fostered understanding across seemingly insurmountable cultural boundaries. Along the way, we will encounter not only advances in problem-solving but also the ethical challenges posed by AI's growing presence in our lives.

In particular, we will turn a critical gaze on the struggle to maintain autonomy and balance responsibility within the increasingly intertwined ecosystems of human cognition and artificial intelligence. To ensure that the AI-augmented world of tomorrow is one endowed with harmony, truth, and intellectual humility, individuals, organizations, and societies must develop strategies to embrace this new frontier effectively.

Our journey thus far has shown us that every facet—indeed every quirk—of human intelligence contains a unique blend of ingenuity and imperfection. As we chart our course towards an era influenced by AI technology, let us hold fast to our newfound humility with open minds and hearts full of wonder.

Our story begins in the early 20th century with Alan Turing, a British mathematician, logician, and codebreaker often heralded as the father of computer science and artificial intelligence. Turing laid the foundations for theoretical computing in his groundbreaking 1936 paper which introduced the concept of a "universal machine" that could simulate any mathematical computation if given a proper set of instructions or "algorithm." The Turing machine, as it would come to be called, was more than merely an abstraction or philosophical curiosity—it foreshadowed today's digital computers.

As World War II raged on, Turing would put his ideas to practical use by designing machines such as the Bombe to break encrypted messages sent by Nazi forces using their Enigma machine. This feat of innovative thinking would later inspire generations of engineers and scientists in their pursuit of a deeper understanding of computation.

It wasn't until several decades later that the field of artificial intelligence would truly take shape. In 1956, researchers John McCarthy, Marvin Minsky, Nathaniel Rochester, and Claude Shannon organized a conference at Dartmouth College which aimed to further research into "thinking machines"—machines that could replicate human intelligence. Thus was born the field known as Artificial Intelligence—a term coined by McCarthy himself.

Throughout the 1950s and '60s, there was a great deal of optimism about what AI could achieve. Symbolic AI, an early approach to artificial intelligence, attempted to model complex human thought processes by incorporating formal logic and symbolic representation. This approach led to the creation of programs that could manipulate language, solve mathematical problems, and replicate elements of human intelligence.

However, it also encountered limitations when trying to capture more intuitive aspects of human reasoning and perception, such as pattern recognition or natural language understanding. Despite the progress made during this era—the so-called "Golden Age" of AI—researchers soon recognized that symbolic AI could not fully emulate human intelligence's subtleties and intricacies.

In parallel with the development of symbolic AI, a separate strand of research was taking root—one grounded in a different vision of how artificial intelligence might draw inspiration from the very wellsprings of human thought: the brain itself. Researchers such as Warren McCulloch and Walter Pitts created the first artificial neural network—a simple computational model simulating neuronal behavior—in 1943. In doing so, they were captivated by the tantalizing prospect that if machines could be designed to mirror some aspect of the brain's structure and function, perhaps they too could learn and adapt over time.

One notable example is Frank Rosenblatt's Perceptron—an early neural network trained to recognize patterns—which became a precursor to modern deep learning systems. Yet despite these initial forays into biologically inspired computing, the promise of neural networks would lie dormant for decades before enjoying a resurgence in the late 20th century.

The reasons for this falling out are multifarious—insufficient computing power, lackluster algorithms, funding constraints—but ultimately boil down to frustration with artificial neural networks' inability to crack complex problems at scale. Learning from data alone seemed like an uphill battle against limited resources.

It wasn't until the 1980s and '90s that a series of innovations in machine learning rekindled excitement around artificial neural networks. Connectionist approaches—which strived to describe cognition through interconnected networks of simple computational units—began to take hold as advancements in computing and algorithmic techniques made it possible to train larger, more expressive models.

As the new millennium approached, a fortuitous convergence of factors breathed life into AI research that had been trudging along at an almost fitful pace. This serendipitous turn of events can be traced to two significant developments: advances in computational power and the proliferation of data.

Throughout the late '90s and 2000s, the rapid acceleration in computing power—as famously predicted by Moore's Law—unleashed a torrent of new opportunities for artificial intelligence. CPUs, or central processing units, have long been the bedrock of computing systems, but they proved to be inefficient for tasks required by machine learning algorithms. Enter GPUs or graphics processing units: originally designed for rendering images in video games, researchers discovered that these processors were ideally suited for handling the parallel computations necessary for training AI models.

Stoked by this innovation, a new enthusiasm built around neural networks as researchers reveled in exploring the potential of AI applied to computer vision, natural language processing, and other feats once considered possible only within the realm of human expertise. By 2012, Geoff Hinton's group had made headlines when their deep neural network won the prestigious ImageNet Challenge—an annual competition that evaluated algorithms' abilities to recognize and classify objects within digital images. With their AI model dramatically outperforming competitors', it was evident that we had entered into a new era with seemingly limitless potential.

However, this newfound prowess in computation alone did not account for AI's renaissance—to appreciate the full picture; one must also consider the data revolution that had been silently brewing beneath society's radar. As internet use skyrocketed worldwide throughout the late '90s and early 2000s, its users were unwittingly churning out enormous volumes of data in every digital nook and cranny by creating emails, texts, tweets, posts, videos, and more. This avalanche of digital detritus would prove to be the motherlode for training AI systems.

In many ways, data is the lifeblood of AI. Just as humans learn from their experiences, so do modern AI algorithms ingest vast arrays of data points in order to hone their skills in tasks as diverse as translation, image recognition, and even medical diagnosis. This concept was perhaps captured best by Chris Anderson's provocative claim in his 2008 Wired article that "with enough data, the numbers speak for themselves." Therein lies the hidden logic of AI's astounding expansion—it was driven by the explosive growth in both computational power and readily accessible large datasets.

But it would be misguided to assume that bigger always equates to better. As with any human endeavor, the process of learning from leviathan-like datasets comes with its own pitfalls and perils—and these must be soberly acknowledged if we are to unlock the true potential of AI without being snared by its many snares.

For instance, drawing solely from large datasets can leave AI models prey to cognitive biases and blind spots inherent within those sources of information—issues that we will explore more deeply in following chapters. In developing sufficiently powerful machines for learning from vast stores of data, researchers must contend with thorny ethical concerns such as privacy violations or algorithmic discrimination.

Moreover, it is essential to remain vigilant against assuming that sheer volume alone will inevitably lead to revelatory insights—lest we succumb to what John Ioannidis termed "the streetlight effect," referring to the anecdotal wisdom that one searches for lost keys under a streetlight not because they are likely to be found there but because that's where it's easiest to see them.

As we forge onwards through this exhilarating odyssey into the eldritch landscape of human cognition and its digital doppelganger, how might we harness these remarkable new tools while remaining grounded in intellectual humility? How can AI alleviate our cognitive blind spots, rather than perpetuating—nay, exacerbating—our faulty perceptions? And most of all, how may we navigate such a world imbued with uncertainties?

31

Enhancing human decision-making

What if there were a way to leverage the powers of AI to identify our biases and help steer us in the direction of more rational thinking? As it turns out, this idea is not only possible—it is already underway.

One of the first steps on this journey is identifying which of our biases pose potential risks, both individually and collectively. It's critical to diagnose when these biases might arise in our decision-making—think of it as a sort of cognitive "radar" system that keeps an eye out for hazardous mental short-cuts hidden amidst an otherwise smooth navigation.

AI developers have been fine-tuning algorithms that can 'sniff out' particular human biases at work—building datasets drawn from diverse sources such as scientific studies, surveys, or even social media interactions that might reveal patterns indicative of bias. By scouring through reams of data representing language, behavior or emotion, these AI models are honing their ability to distinguish between genuine insights and pitfalls that lead us astray.

Consider the challenge posed by confirmation bias—the proclivity for gravitating towards evidence that bolsters our preconceived notions while discounting any disconfirming information. This hardwired 'mental glitch' has led many brilliant minds down the path of faulty conclusions and hasty generalizations. With AI's help, we can craft systems designed to detect when someone is falling prey to confirmation bias by offering alternate interpretations or data points that run counter to prevailing assumptions. This serves both as a gentle reminder for open-mindedness and an instigator for diverse perspectives in intellectual discourse.

Another compelling example lies within the realm of medicine, where several lives may hang in the balance of a single clinical decision. Medical professionals are not immune to the same cognitive traps that befall laypersons, with biases like anchoring, availability, or representativeness influencing diagnoses and treatment plans even among experts. In recent years, AI-powered decision support systems have begun to make their presence felt in fields such as radiology, pathology, and oncology   through these systems, it becomes possible for doctors to access additional valuable information that diverts them from common cognitive traps.

It's important to recognize that mitigating cognitive biases is not merely about augmenting individual thought processes but also transforming institutional decision-making at large. Organizations can deploy AI-driven tools to predict when certain biases might come into play — for example, by analyzing past business decisions or identifying problematic patterns that suggest potential system-wide biases.

AI may also be enlisted in efforts to diversify hiring processes and increase inclusivity in the workplace—counteracting unconscious biases that stand as barriers to entry for underrepresented demographics. AI-enabled recruitment solutions can assist HR teams in identifying patterns of inadvertent discrimination throughout a company's hiring practices while offering remedial insights into developing more inclusive policies.

Just as crucially, educators may utilize AI in guiding students through an expansive understanding of the world around them, equipping the next generation with robust mental frameworks necessary for navigating a complex, endlessly evolving global landscape. For instance, AI-based tutoring systems can help nurture intellectual humility by revealing alternative viewpoints and contextualizing prevailing assumptions within broader streams of thought.

Having said all this, it would be imprudent not to acknowledge the potential pitfalls awaiting us down such a path. While AI can offer invaluable assistance in rooting out bespoke instances where our cognitive machinery fails us, we must remain ever-vigilant against complacency—a belief that simply offloading our thinking onto algorithms will liberate us from all manner of fallacies and faults.

The risks present myriad challenges: What if the very AI models tasked with counteracting human biases reflect those biases in their programming or data? What if, amidst a thicket of false positives or negatives, we become blindsided to our own biases? And how can we remain agile in embracing dissenting perspectives while ensuring a constructive and respectful exchange with our robotic interlocutors?

It is vital to understand that AI, like any other tool, is only as effective in mitigating cognitive biases as the humans that wield it. This raises a crucial question: If mitigating cognitive biases through AI hinges upon the due diligence of its creators and users, then might there be more fruitful ways to imbue these same skills directly within ourselves as individuals, educators or institutions? Might we consider enhancing our cognitive radar system—an ability to predict and pre-empt problematic patterns in thought—through more human-centered endeavors?

As valuable as it is to equip our minds with strategies for identifying and mitigating biases, fostering intellectual humility requires more than simply steering clear of mental traps. To embrace a truly humble mindset, we must actively engage in seeking diverse opinions, challenging our assumptions, and remaining receptive to learning from the intellectual journeys of others. But in a world inundated with voices clamoring for our attention, where do we start?

Enter the concept of personalized recommendations, harnessing AI's potential to deliver customized suggestions tailored to individual needs, preferences, and contexts. Whether it be browsing through a seemingly infinite library of books, articles or podcasts, sifting through an overwhelming volume of online resources or obtaining real-time feedback on our work, AI-enabled personalization can equip us with valuable tools that help cultivate intellectual humility.

Imagine an algorithm that monitors your reading habits—carefully observing patterns of interests and preconceptions—to provide you with an assortment of curated content offering alternative perspectives on a particular topic. How might this nudge those seeds of intellectual curiosity into blossoming into vibrant new insights? Or consider a personalized learning platform capable of evaluating your strengths and weaknesses—adapting its instruction to challenge you in areas that require growth while bolstering existing expertise.

But let's not restrict ourselves to mere skill development—imagine the transformational possibilities offered by AI when applied to enrich personal relationships and communication patterns. A system designed to closely study the contours of conversation—identifying trends indicative of either stubbornness or openness—might supply tactful prompts or suggestions encouraging individuals to question their assumptions or seek out alternative viewpoints.

Unlocking potential like this doesn't just call for taming biases—it demands the fortitude necessary for engaging in rigorous self-reflection. By distilling nuanced patterns in our personal conversations and embracing those perspectives previously overlooked or obscured, such AI-powered systems draw us closer to the foundational humility required for robust dialogue.

Delving further within the realm of possibilities, envision an AI-powered personal assistant that intelligently guides you through moments of decision-making by first prompting you to consider a diverse array of perspectives. These virtual interlocutors might offer tailored insights on the role of cognitive biases or emotional factors in your deliberations, thus fostering intellectual humility alongside more rational and level-headed problem-solving.

Beyond individual lenses, one cannot ignore the prospect that AI may shape our social interactions in ways which promote humility and understanding within broader human networks. Picture an online platform—much like today's social media sphere—that elevates voices espousing tolerance and thoughtfulness while attenuating noise and echo chambers. These open-minded realms contrast sharply with the closed circuits of ideological conformity that often emerge on the contemporary digital landscape.

An essential caveat to heed in discussing these proposals is the recognition that genuine intellectual humility cannot be fully outsourced to technological intermediaries. While AI can certainly propel us towards embracing diverse viewpoints and broadening our horizons, there remains a crucial role entrusted solely to human agency: the ability to ask questions that probe deeper and resist complacency-driven convictions.

As we plot this trajectory towards greater receptiveness, it becomes increasingly important to consider how our own dispositions play a part in navigating this journey. True intellectual humility calls for individuals ready to embrace not only novel perspectives but also potential fallibility—cognizant of the transient and limited nature of their current understanding.

While AI-based personalization holds much promise for fostering intellectual humility both individually and collectively, we must recognize the limitations inherent within its use. Awareness of such constraints empowers us to strike a balance—a symbiotic relationship wherein AI nudges us toward fresh vantage points while we remain vigilant against any false sense of omniscience proffered by our mechanized companions.

One of the most potent ways in which AI can contribute to our collective journey towards intellectual humility is by uncovering obscured patterns within vast amounts of data that might otherwise elude human perception. These hidden patterns have the power to challenge deeply entrenched preconceptions—ushering us towards transformative moments of enlightenment that defy our expectations.

It is no secret that human reasoning can be swayed by a variety of factors, ranging from cognitive biases to emotional responses and societal influences. Our cognitive radar often has blind spots, skewing perception and impeding our ability to discern hidden connections in the torrent of data surrounding us. Yet, with their capacity for unbiased analysis and rapid pattern recognition, AI systems are uniquely positioned to deliver precisely those insights we may least expect.

Envision an AI-driven research platform that scans multiple datasets—spanning domains such as economics, healthcare, and climate change—to reveal hidden interdependencies and unanticipated implications across seemingly unrelated fields. By exposing these complex relationships, AI-generated insights might lead experts to question long-held beliefs and re-evaluate assumptions in light of previously unseen correlations.

One notable example of this phenomenon occurs when examining the intersection between mental health and traffic congestion. On the surface, these issues appear entirely separate. However, a meticulous examination of data reveals a surprising connection: as traffic congestion increases in urban areas, so does the incidence of stress and anxiety disorders among drivers. The AI-powered revelation underscores an urgency for policymakers to reassess their understanding and response to both challenges within an intricately interwoven context.

Delving beyond matters concerning policy adaptations or disciplinary boundaries—a realm where AI delivers profound value lies in facilitating personal growth by confronting us with perspectives that dismantle insular worldviews. An AI-enabled tool might identify subtle threads weaving through historical narratives or cultural expressions which precipitate momentous shifts in perspective—for example, revealing how forces we may perceive as distinct (such as urbanization, climate change, or technological advancement) are intimately entwined.

Grasping these interconnected strands can lead to a deep appreciation for the impact individuals have on one another—a sentiment that fosters empathetic communication and an inclusive environment.

In yet another domain, AI-managed social experiments could offer powerful insights into the effects of human behavior in diverse contexts. By simulating various scenarios and potential consequences, AI tools might present us with counter-intuitive findings that contradict conventional wisdom. Stumbling upon such contrary knowledge presents a prime opportunity to cultivate intellectual humility by questioning our understanding and considering alternative explanations before jumping to conclusions.

But identifying obscured patterns is only the first step—translating these discoveries into palpable actions is crucial in nurturing intellectual humility. An environment enriched with AI-based systems capable of discerning connections beyond human reach retains immense potential for growth, but it also beckons a willingness on our part to absorb these unexpected lessons.

In this context, both the AI system and its human user engage in an elaborate dance—one where technology presents us with new knowledge while we grapple with reconciling it with prior beliefs. Fostering intellectual humility is not solely about uncovering divergent perspectives or hidden relationships—the process requires humans to embrace newfound knowledge with open-mindedness and relinquish certainty in favor of continual learning.

Throughout this vast terrain of possibilities, the central challenge lies within our response: How do we absorb these AI-guided discoveries and allow them to reshape our thoughts? How do we wield this technology's potential without surrendering our sense of agency or responsibility? The answer rests in embracing intellectual humility as a cornerstone of growth—a mindset that perceives complexity as an integral facet of existence rather than a hindrance to be conquered.

Ultimately, AI-powered revelations of obscured patterns reveal the limitations of our own understanding while illuminating pathways towards increased knowledge and personal growth. These discoveries—unexpected though they may be—provide fertile ground in which to seed humility. However, it is up to us to choose whether we tend to the soil and willingly reap the transformative fruits of our intellectual harvest.

32

Augmenting collective intelligence

We now turn our lens towards the application of AI in augmenting collective intelligence—a dimension that merits profound attention given its impact on the fabric of human collaboration. By employing AI systems in breaking the barriers of groupthink, we can expand our capacity for tapping into diverse perspectives and effectively harness the power of collective intelligence to achieve unprecedented breakthroughs.

Groupthink, a term coined by psychologist Irving Janis in 1972, refers to the tendency for individuals within a cohesive group to prioritize conformity over independent thought, leading to decisions that lack holistic evaluation. This phenomenon can stem from factors such as a desire to maintain harmony within the group or an inclination to reinforce one's own beliefs rather than welcoming dissenting opinions. The result: suboptimal decisions guided by narrow perspectives, flawed reasoning, and unaddressed biases.

AI technology holds strong promise in helping us identify and dismantle these invisible constraints on collective intelligence. An AI-driven collaboration platform could monitor group dynamics in real-time by gauging factors like conformity levels, sentiment polarity, diversity of opinions expressed—and ultimately generate gentle nudges guiding participants towards balanced conversations that reduce echo chambers. By being attuned to both individual cognitive tendencies and emergent patterns within group interactions, AI systems can generate nuanced guidance facilitating more inclusive decision-making processes.

To illustrate this point, imagine a UN-sponsored climate summit where leaders and advocates from across the world convene to address pressing global issues. In such high-stakes discussions where numerous personal, national, and cultural biases might intertwine, an AI-enabled tool working behind the scenes could aid in weaving together disparate threads— e.g., highlighting overlooked correlations between regional policy implemen-tations or underscoring corroborated research findings that cut through emotionally-charged disagreements. Through targeted recommendations that combine contextual understanding with unbiased analysis, AI stands poised to engender courageous explorations beyond the comfortable bounds of shared assumptions.

This approach would not simply entail identifying inconsistencies or chal-lenging ideas within group discussions; rather, it must also encourage partic-ipants to actively confront and reevaluate the assumptions embedded in their beliefs. An AI-driven support system can catalyze such a transformation by taking on the role of a Socratic mentor—an insightful presence ready to prod us with thought-provoking reflections, fostering intellectual humility while instilling an aspirational drive to discover truth.

In business settings, AI-guided collaboration tools could detect when the discussion is dominated by a select few (perhaps those wielding senior roles or displaying high levels of confidence) while others are being sidelined. Consequently, these tools would trigger prompts that foster horizontal communication structure and ensure diverse voices can find their foot-ing—breaking the tendency towards groupthink without undermining interpersonal rapport.

Another aspect of quelling groupthink pertains to sharpening receptivity to external input. Expertise-driven communities—especially within scientific domains—are often insular, grappling with highly specialized niche knowledge and skeptical about "outsider" perspectives. However, forging innovative solutions often demands cross-disciplinary understanding and refining the capacity for entering new paradigms.

AI advances in natural language understanding can play a pivotal role in bridging these disciplinary gaps. Leveraging advanced algorithms, we can design dynamic systems that transform information into accessible narratives—transcending jargon boundaries among disciplines or cultural language barriers hindering global collaboration. As William Butler Yeats once astutely noted: "Education is not filling a bucket but igniting a fire." Thus, an AI-facilitated learning environment might dismantle informational silos not by amassing increasingly large repositories of specialist knowledge but by sparking curiosity-driven explorations between complementary fields.

As participants in collaborative settings grow increasingly conversant with adopting multiple perspectives, they become better equipped to abandon groupthink tendencies—embracing cognitive diversity as an engine for innovation rather than as an existential threat to long-held convictions.

Yet, there lies an overarching challenge that resists easy solutions—the delicate balancing act of harnessing the power of AI without succumbing to its potential pitfalls. As much as AI systems hold the potential to expand our collaborative horizons, there exists an attendant risk that we might begin to over-rely on these tools—possibly devolving into groupthink orchestrated by algorithms.

This concern sparks pressing questions surrounding the intersection of AI and intellectual integrity: If we delegate portions of decision-making to artificial systems, how might we retain our position as active agents within this process? How do we guard against the possibility of replacing one form of groupthink with another, perpetuated by unquestioned reliance on algorithmic insight?

The answer, once again, lies in nurturing a culture infused with intellectual humility. We must ensure that AI serves as a partner that enhances human ingenuity rather than a crutch that dispenses prescribed knowledge. By cultivating an ongoing dialogue that fosters deep reflection and challenges algorithmic suggestions when necessary, we remain in control—steering the course towards informed decisions rather than relinquishing ownership to machines.

As we navigate the complex world of human collaboration, a striking dimension emerges: the challenge of enabling effective communication across cultural, linguistic, and disciplinary boundaries. The potential of reaching new heights by leveraging diverse views is sometimes overshadowed by the difficulties in overcoming these barriers. However, AI technology offers promising solutions in addressing this age-old conundrum.

Language lies at the heart of any attempt to foster an open dialogue between individuals from varying backgrounds. Skilled human translators have long functioned as invaluable resources, bridging gaps between linguistic communities and facilitating mutual understanding. That said, simultaneous translation within real-time conversations—where each interlocutor speaks from their unique cultural and intellectual context—is a challenging feat even for seasoned linguists.

This is where AI comes into play: advancements in natural language processing (NLP) offer impressive gains when it comes to decoding syntactic nuances and semantic subtleties across various languages. Leveraging machine learning algorithms trained on vast multilingual datasets—including idiomatic expressions, metaphorical language, and culturally-specific vocabulary—AI systems can provide increasingly accurate translations that enable deeper understanding between parties.

But what about misunderstandings that have less to do with linguistic differences and more to do with underlying assumptions or differing values? Here too, AI has the potential to help bridge these complex cultural divides. Algorithms might be capable of detecting potential areas of friction in conversations—offering suggestions for alternative phrasings or gentle reframing that avoids inadvertently offending or alienating others.

Moreover, fostering empathy and understanding between conflicting parties is critical in dealing with cultural tensions that might arise during global collaborations—an area where AI-driven programs have shown remarkable promise. For instance, digital platforms that simulate interpersonal interactions can utilize emotion recognition technologies to capture subtle nuances in body language and facial expressions—providing users with real-time insights into their conversation partners' emotional states. This level of sensitivity can enhance participants' awareness of social cues and encourage thoughtful engagement—building a foundation for lasting cooperative ties.

To move beyond language and address the challenges posed by disciplinary boundaries, we can take advantage of AI's ability to parse through vast amounts of specialized knowledge and synthesize it into accessible narratives. By doing so, diverse experts can find common ground without diluting their unique insights; rather, they are empowered to forge creative connections that propel innovation forward.

Picture an astrophysicist, an environmental policymaker, and an urban planner collaborating on tackling climate change within their respective domains. While each of them brings specialized knowledge to the table, they might struggle to communicate effectively due to the technical jargon and divergent perspectives that mark their distinct disciplines. In such cases, AI-powered tools can deconstruct complex concepts into relatable examples and analogies, allowing various stakeholders to appreciate each other's viewpoints without becoming mired in the intricacies of unfamiliar terminology.

This process goes beyond mere translation—it involves crafting meaningful representations of core ideas that resonate with individuals hailing from distinct intellectual traditions. Weaving together diverse threads of expertise requires not only linguistic finesse but also an understanding of how these different fields intersect—a task that neural networks trained on cross-disciplinary data are uniquely poised to accomplish.

As an example, one could envision an AI-driven system that recognizes burgeoning areas of interdisciplinary collaboration—then curates targeted learning resources based on individual participants' backgrounds and interests—such as concise explainers on systems thinking for geneticists or brief workshops for engineers tackling ecological challenges. In this manner, AI systems could function as virtual mentors that foster curiosity-driven exploration between complementary fields—simultaneously cultivating intellectual humility and paving the way for collective growth.

At its essence, enabling effective communication across cultural, linguistic, and disciplinary boundaries is fundamentally about authenticity—creating space where individuals can express themselves openly while being receptive to alternative beliefs that challenge their existing worldviews. When AI tools are synergized with human ingenuity—one complementing the other—the result has the potential to be transformative.

That said, it's crucial to acknowledge the perennial nature of human bias and ensure that AI-driven platforms designed to tackle communication barriers don't inadvertently fall prey to these same pitfalls. Mitigating algorithmic bias and preventing discrimination against certain groups or perspectives is key in designing AI systems that facilitate truly inclusive exchanges.

The importance of such a cautious approach comes into sharper focus when considering potential adverse consequences. Imagine an AI-facilitated conversation where biases encoded within the algorithm result in communication skewed towards certain cultural or demographic groups. In such cases, the possibility of exacerbating existing divides instead of bridging them looms large—a danger we must actively engage with as we explore AI's role in transcending boundaries.

Yet, when wielded mindfully, AI holds immense promise in facilitating intellectual connections across myriad chasms of understanding—bridges that span not only languages but cultural mores and disciplinary frontiers as well. As actors from distinct corners of the globe harness the power vested within these synergistic partnerships, new avenues for global collaboration come to life—ushering in what could well become an era defined by heightened empathy, profound cross-disciplinary insights, and shared reverence for the potential lies locked within our brilliant yet fallible minds.

In our increasingly polarized world, harnessing empathy and understanding bears even greater significance—at the individual, community, and international levels alike. AI technology, with its sophisticated capacity to process human emotions and complex interplays of perspectives, holds great potential in fostering these essentials of mutual understanding among discordant parties.

Conflict resolution often begins with acknowledging the interplay of various components that contribute to it—whether rooted in emotional experiences or differing ideologies. AI-enhanced systems are uniquely poised to help by shedding light on the intricate patterns and forces shaping these divergent stances. By comparing linguistic cues, analyzing body language, and synthesizing vast amounts of data from a rich tapestry of sources, AI tools can offer fresh insights into the multifaceted nature of conflicts that may have eluded traditional approaches.

Consider the role AI-driven sentiment analysis might play in this context.

Sentiment analysis algorithms can process textual data from an extensive range of sources—such as social media posts or political manifestos—and perform large-scale identification of emotionally-charged topics within them. Armed with this information, intermediaries or negotiators could be attuned to the nuances underpinning two opposing sides' deeply-held beliefs—allowing for more targeted and empathetic interventions when bridging gaps between disputants.

Beyond understanding the underlying sentiments at play in conflicts, AI can also foster empathy by simulating interpersonal interactions more authentically than ever before. Virtual reality (VR) simulations combined with advanced emotion recognition technologies offer fertile ground for immersive experiences—wherein users are exposed to alternative perspectives in emotionally charged contexts while receiving feedback on their own responses.

Picture a scenario where conflicting parties partake in a series of expertly-crafted VR simulations that enable them to virtually step into each other's lives: individuals swapping roles while engaging in firsthand encounters with their perceived foes' struggles, triumphs, and aspirations. Participants might find themselves viscerally immersed within the throes of their counterparts' lived experiences—such as a community leader navigating a fractious political climate or a parent striving to provide for their family amid economic strife. Over time, these AI-driven immersive experiences, coupled with real-time emotion analysis tools to guide users through the unfolding narrative, could foster empathy by revealing shared humanity beneath outward differences.

Empathy, however, is just the first stage in resolving conflicts. AI's true potential unfolds when it is employed to craft creative resolutions that defy conventional thinking and challenge entrenched positions. Here, multi-agent artificial intelligence—where multiple AI-powered entities negotiate on behalf of humans—shows much promise. By utilizing intelligent agents programmed to optimize positive-sum outcomes and prevent zero-sum thinking, these systems offer a novel way of brokering compromises between individuals or groups locked in animosity.

As an example, one could envision AI-driven algorithms collaboratively crafting negotiation strategies by sifting through myriad alternative resolutions proposed by individual stakeholders—each agent objectively weighing the pros and cons of these suggestions against pre-established criteria that serve collective welfare. By homing in on solutions that transcend traditional 'us-versus-them' dichotomies, AI-powered mediation can expose the latent commonalities linking seemingly incompatible viewpoints—outcomes rooted in a profound understanding of what truly matters to those embroiled within conflicts.

It is important to note that the success of AI-mediated conflict resolution hinges upon embedding ethical principles into these systems and maintaining transparency regarding eventual recommendations—clarifying how particular conclusions were reached and why certain values were prioritized over others. Earning mutual trust is vital when broaching sensitive issues within contentious dialogues.

Moreover, fostering empathy and understanding among discordant parties would be incomplete without addressing the presence of underlying systemic issues that fuel conflicts in the first place. Here again, AI has a role to play—as both a diagnostic tool and an aid in formulating remedial measures.

Imagine a city grappling with social unrest amidst acute socioeconomic disparities. An AI-driven approach to this challenge might begin by analyzing geographical data alongside indicators such as income, education, employment, health, and crime levels—unearthing trends and correlations that delve deeper into the roots of discord. By identifying the interwoven factors that breed disparities and underlying tensions, AI can provide civic authorities with evidence-based insights on which structural changes might alleviate the strife. Further, these systems could also support participatory urban planning initiatives—inviting citizens to share their ideas in devising and appraising urban interventions capable of transforming contested spaces into equitable social landscapes.

In essence, fostering empathy and understanding among conflicting parties with the help of AI tools begins by illuminating the values, feelings, and systemic forces shaping the contours of these disputes. By leveraging innovative technologies such as sentiment analysis, VR simulations powered by emotion recognition, multi-agent negotiations, and large-scale data synthesis—AI can shed light on myriad connections linking seemingly disparate entities while charting pathways towards resolution within an empathetic and just framework.

However, we have to recognize that AI-driven conflict resolution is not without its potential pitfalls. Any system that encompasses emotionally charged issues or contains ingrained biases will need judicious countermeasures to ensure fairness. Strict monitoring of AI-generated recommendations for ethicality, objectivity, transparency, as well as cultural and demographic inclusivity is imperative if we are to wield this powerful technology responsibly.

$$33$$

Empowering scientific inquiry

In discussing the potential of AI to foster empathy and understanding, we have touched upon its capacity to transcend human cognitive biases in the pursuit of truth. Now, let us delve further into how machine learning can give a crucial push to scientific research—a domain where the quest for knowledge and clarity has always fueled progress.

It is an established truism that science thrives on rigorous experimentation, extensive data analysis, and continuous testing of prevailing hypotheses. In the face of complex, multidimensional problems that call for creative solutions and evidence-based insights, machine learning emerges as a powerful ally. By automating routine tasks, discerning subtle patterns across vast datasets, and drawing connections between seemingly unrelated phenomena, AI-driven systems offer scientists new resources for faster discovery.

Consider first the possibilities raised by automation within scientific research. With advancements in AI-controlled robotics and computer vision technology, these systems have transformed laboratory workflows: conducting experiments, analyzing samples, even generating novel hypotheses—effectively relieving researchers from mundane tasks while granting more time for idea development and contemplation. This shift frees up substantial cognitive bandwidth; as they are no longer bound to repetitive routines, curious minds are unleashed to explore fresh perspectives and tackle uncharted challenges.

Beyond automating tasks traditionally shouldered by human scientists, machine learning makes its mark through sheer scale and computational power—evident when one marvels at its prowess in combing through colossal datasets with often astonishing precision. AI's ability to capture relevant findings within vast seas of information is particularly valuable in domains such as genomics or neuroscience; these disciplines grapple with enormous piles of data and demand considerable attention for discerning significant patterns or correlations.

Take the realm of genomics as an example. The field has witnessed a plethora of new discoveries since scientists first mapped out the human genome—an undertaking that took well over a decade. Ongoing breakthroughs now accompany rapid advances in DNA sequencing technology: where millions of genes are revealed daily with potential links to myriad medical conditions and diseases. Here, machine learning algorithms stand as indispensable tools for sifting this ocean of genetic data—identifying genes linked to certain ailments, unearthing novel drug targets, even generating suggestions for tailoring treatment plans that suit an individual's unique genomic makeup.

In a similar vein, the possibilities engendered by machine learning in neuroscience are nothing short of awe-inspiring. Consider the challenges involved in deciphering the workings of the human brain—a dense network composed of billions of neurons connected through trillions of intricate synapses. Traditional, manual analysis of such data would be impossibly time-consuming; AI-driven tools emerge as crucial allies in detecting minute patterns and mapping functional connections within this vast landscape.

Illustrative examples abound, ranging from AI systems that examine countless electrophysiological recordings in search of new information on cellular signaling pathways, to those that analyze voluminous MRI or fMRI data—uncovering correlations between specific brain activity patterns and cognitive functions or mental health conditions. Together, these AI-driven milestones have propelled our understanding of the brain by leaps and bounds.

Let us not overlook the role machine learning can play in facilitating collaboration across disparate domains. Oftentimes, innovative solutions stem from combining diverse scientific disciplines—a task well-suited to AI's capacity for seamlessly weaving different strands of thought together. With sophisticated algorithms that parse terabytes upon terabytes of research articles—scouring literature databases that span fields as wide-ranging as astronomy and zoology—scientists can unearth unexpected associations and interdisciplinary insights.

As an example, picture an ecology researcher seeking to probe the underlying reasons behind a decline in migratory bird populations. Utilizing machine learning algorithms capable of mining large volumes of publications from fields such as climatology or air pollution science, this scientist might discover unforeseen patterns at play—clarifying how environmental pressures unique to particular regions intersect with avian migration behavior. Moreover, these same algorithmic tools might steer our researcher towards burgeoning trends of research interest, thereby elucidating potential collaborative opportunities with far-flung colleagues.

Opponents of AI's encroachment into scientific inquiry may argue that the human touch—intuition, creativity, and boundless curiosity—cannot be supplanted by machines. Contrary to this popular misconception, the true beauty of machine learning lies not in outright supplanting the human mind, but in expanding its horizons and augmenting its abilities by offering novel perspectives and resources. When we form genuine partnerships between scientists and intelligent machines, we grant ourselves access to an intellectual playground brimming with unforeseen discoveries.

It is tempting to lay focus predominantly on the incremental achievements wrought by AI-driven technologies, as noted above. Still, equal attention ought to be paid to more revolutionary transformations—disruptions that fundamentally alter how we approach scientific discovery itself. Notable examples include the growing field of quantum computing, which promises to redefine computational power and efficiency or projects like OpenAI's GPT-3, an advanced language model with myriad applications in natural language processing or reinforcement learning.

These cutting-edge innovations harbor potential for unleashing seismic shifts within established fields or entirely birthing new ones—compelling us to question long-held assumptions while striving towards a deeper comprehension of our world. In essence, these projects exemplify the profound implications that machine learning holds when steered consciously toward accelerating scientific research.

Recognizing and celebrating these potentialities should not be done without caution, however. Just as we have emphasized throughout this book: the use of AI warrants ethical considerations and steadfast monitoring to manage pervasive biases or unintended consequences stemming from its application. But by forging ahead with vigilance, guided by relentlessly curious intellects equipped with powerful computational tools borne from sophisticated artificial intelligence systems—we unlock fresh arenas for unrivaled collaboration in understanding our universe.

Having surveyed the vastness of AI's influence on scientific discovery and touched upon cutting-edge innovations, it is instructive to turn to specific instances where machines have played a pivotal role in advancing our understanding of complex problems. To see collaborative problem-solving with AI in action, let's delve into case studies from diverse fields such as physics, biology, and beyond.

It is a curious quirk of history that physics, the most exact and mathematical of the sciences, has become a fertile ground for artful creativity and daring leaps of the imagination. Hence, it seems fitting that AI and machine learning have come to inhabit ever more significant roles within this domain. In particular, astrophysics stands as an exemplary case study of AI's collaboration with human experts in solving cosmic mysteries.

A striking testament to the power of such partnerships lies in our greatly improved grasp of exoplanetary systems—remote celestial realms characterized by planets orbiting distant stars. The search for new worlds beyond our solar system—a task intimately tied to the broader quest for understanding life's origins and its potential ubiquity—has seen profound impacts from AI-driven methods. These systems have enabled scientists to analyze astronomical data faster and more accurately than ever before.

Consider NASA's Kepler mission: launched in 2009, this space observatory was tasked with identifying Earth-like planets by monitoring minute fluctuations in stellar brightness caused by orbiting exoplanets. Over its nine-year lifespan, Kepler observed over 500,000 stars and generated massive volumes of data ripe for analysis. By combining advanced machine learning algorithms with the expertise of astronomers, researchers have thus far confirmed more than 2,800 previously undiscovered exoplanets.

Indeed, among the myriad discoveries made possible by such collaborations are fascinating phenomena like "hot Jupiters" or "Super-Earths"—terms describing exotic planetary bodies undreamed-of merely decades ago. As we peer deeper into the cosmos with advanced telescopes like the James Webb Space Telescope, scheduled for launch in the near future, our understanding of these far-ranging planetary systems will likely continue to expand—propelled, in no small part, by AI-animated human curiosity.

Turning now to the biological sciences, we witness ample evidence of fruitful collaborations between machine learning systems and human researchers. To appreciate this symbiosis in action, consider recent advances made in protein folding—a complex biophysical process crucial to understanding life at the molecular level yet notoriously challenging to decipher.

For decades, scientists have grappled with the "protein folding problem"—predicting a protein's three-dimensional structure based solely on its sequence of amino acids. Accurate predictions bear transformative implications for drug discovery and development; they enable us to understand how a protein functions within cells and how its structure might be targeted with specific medications.

Enter DeepMind's AlphaFold—an AI system that married cutting-edge deep learning techniques with human expertise to unravel the problem at an unprecedented speed and resolution. In 2020, AlphaFold achieved a stunning breakthrough when it produced highly accurate protein folding predictions during a competition known as CASP (Critical Assessment of Structure Prediction). This feat heralded a dramatic acceleration in our understanding of proteins and opened new doors for drug development—a prime example of AI's potential to drive scientific progress when joined with human minds.

Our final case study carries us from the physical cosmos into the abstract realm of mathematics. Here too, we find compelling instances of collaborative problem-solving between intelligent machines and their human counterparts. Among the most striking exemplars is Eureka: an AI-driven system developed by researchers at MIT that blends symbolic reasoning with deep learning algorithms.

In 2019, Eureka made headlines when it autonomously generated a groundbreaking conjecture surrounding graph coloring—a longstanding area of mathematical inquiry involving maps, networks, and allocation problems. Impressively, it took mere hours for Eureka to scan previously published literature on graph theory while formulating this novel conjecture—a feat that no lone researcher could have accomplished with similar alacrity.

By offering a fresh perspective on complex mathematical problems, AI-powered systems like Eureka hold potential as invaluable collaborators for mathematicians worldwide. With both brute computational force and capacity for algorithmic imagination, such tools forge an undeniable synergy between the creative genius of mathematicians and razor-sharp artificial intelligence.

In each of these case studies, we witness the power of collaboration between scientists and advanced machine learning systems. Through diverse applications ranging from studying cosmic phenomena to unraveling molecular intricacies or delving into arcane mathematical complexities, these partnerships have engendered monumental strides in our understanding of pertinent issues. Yet, one caveat must resound: the true strength of these collaborations stems not from AI systems supplanting human curiosity and creativity, but from their capacity to augment those very qualities nurtured within dedicated researchers.

The examples we've explored here represent merely a sliver of the vast array of problems tackled through collaborative problem-solving with machines. Indeed, throughout the sciences, evidence abounds testifying to the transformative impact of technologies such as neural networks and deep learning systems when combined with passionate human intellects.

At this juncture, we find ourselves beholding not only the promise but also realizing tangible positive outcomes stemming from the embrace of AI-enhanced collaboration within scientific inquiry. Without sacrificing our unique perspectives or shying away from ethical considerations surrounding these intelligent tools, we can continue to invest in truly revolutionary research that transcends traditional boundaries—effectively unlocking more profound understandings of our world and ourselves therein.

As we have seen, the partnership between human experts and artificial intelligence has resulted in significant advancements across a wide range of domains. In each instance, the ability of AI to handle immense volumes of data serves as a defining factor for success. Owing to the rapid increase in the availability and size of datasets, humans alone struggle to sift through this information treasure trove. It is in such contexts that AI systems excel—not merely by brute force but with a flair for uncovering patterns otherwise obscured from human understanding.

One of the most salient examples of this phenomenon can be observed in the realm of climate science—a field that has increasingly relied on artificial intelligence and machine learning to process massive datasets and uncover valuable insights. Given the stakes, our capacity to adapt to an unpredictable future depends heavily on our understanding of pending climatic shifts.

For millennia, weather patterns have preoccupied us—from ancient civilizations' desperate prayers for rain to farmers poring over almanacs. Today, climate researchers equipped with sophisticated tools stand poised to illuminate impending global transformations even beyond meteorological trends.

Consider the pioneering project Climate TRACE: an international initiative harnessing machine learning techniques to predict greenhouse gas emissions at an unprecedented level of detail. By accessing real-time data from remote sensing devices—including satellites, weather stations, and internet-connected instruments—the project aims to provide accurate, fine-grained estimates of worldwide emissions.

Such insights are crucial for creating more effective climate policies and innovative solutions. Equipped with reliable emissions data at an industry-by-industry or even factory-by-factory scale, policymakers can identify problem areas and prioritize interventions accordingly. The potential applications extend far beyond simple policymaking too; detailed insight about carbon footprints allows individuals to make more informed choices regarding their consumption habits and lifestyle changes.

Similarly, AI-driven data analysis exposes previously unnoticed correlations within datasets related to natural disasters and extreme weather events. While climate scientists are no strangers to deciphering connections between disparate variables—such as ice melt, sea level rise, and ocean currents—the sheer scale of available data often places limitations on their insights. With the assistance of machine learning algorithms, researchers can process these colossal datasets, revealing hidden trends and enhancing our understanding of climate change.

AI has also demonstrated potential in tackling a key challenge for the renewable energy sector: forecasting the availability of solar and wind resources. Since electricity grids must maintain an optimal balance between supply and demand—one that is constantly shifting due to rates of consumption and fluctuations in renewable power generation—predicting this balance is crucial for ensuring grid stability and reducing energy waste.

By employing deep learning models trained on vast datasets, AI systems can forecast sunlight availability, wind speeds, and other weather parameters with remarkable accuracy. Such forecasts empower grid operators to make informed, real-time decisions about how much power to generate from different sources. With higher-resolution forecasts in hand, we are better equipped to integrate renewable power into our energy systems—an essential step toward a sustainable future.

Outside climatic investigations, AI's ability to handle large datasets has propelled critical discoveries across various domains. In the realm of medical research—a field where the stakes are undeniably high—such breakthroughs include revolutionizing our understanding of human biology and leading us towards a new era of personalized medicine.

Modern cancer treatment has made substantial gains thanks to advances in genomics and targeted therapies; however, determining optimal treatments for individual patients remains a challenge. The sheer complexity and size of genomic datasets mean that piecing together actionable information is beyond the capacity of most clinicians.

Enter Watson for Genomics: a system that processes vast datasets encompassing scientific literature, genetic tests, clinical trials data, patient medical records, and more to identify treatment options tailored to individual cancer patients' specific circumstances. By doing so, this AI-driven technology empowers clinicians to make more accurate decisions about targeted therapies—a boon for patients and a reaffirmation of AI's potential to propel personalized medicine.

This is by no means an exhaustive account of the ways in which AI excels at processing vast datasets to unearth insights that might otherwise elude us. Time and again, across multiple disciplines—geology, epidemiology, economics—we find instances where combining astute human expertise with the computational prowess of machine learning algorithms yields transformative breakthroughs.

34

Navigating ethical challenges

While the integration of AI systems into our decision-making processes can significantly help overcome inherent cognitive biases, it is crucial to remember that these models are not immune to limitations themselves. Algorithms, after all, are designed by humans, reflecting their creators' assumptions, biases, and belief systems. Moreover, machine learning algorithms are trained on large-scale datasets collected from human-generated inputs: data imbued with the very prejudices we seek to avoid.

Consequently, for AI to become a reliable partner in our quest for intellectual humility and enhanced understanding of the truth, we must address algorithmic bias—a term that encompasses both conscious and unconscious biases embedded within artificial intelligence systems.

To appreciate the consequences of unchecked algorithmic biases, one need look no further than the realm of facial recognition technology. Numerous studies have demonstrated that various facial recognition algorithms consistently display higher error rates when analyzing images of darker-skinned people—an alarming finding with dire implications across sectors, such as criminal law enforcement and hiring practices.

The root cause of racial discrimination embedded in AI can often be traced back to training datasets. If an AI system is predominantly exposed to images featuring light-skinned faces through the training process, its ability to generalize effectively is subsequently hampered. The system becomes biased due to inadequate exposure to diverse data points—mirroring broader concerns about prejudice and exclusion prevalent in human society.

In this context, mitigating algorithmic bias is a two-fold process. First, we must actively strive for diversity and inclusivity in our training data. By ensuring that machine learning algorithms are exposed to a wide array of data points representative of different ethnicities, genders, socio-economic backgrounds, and other pertinent factors, we set them up for success.

Moreover, diversity should not be confined merely within datasets; organizations involved in AI development must strive for diversity among their teams as well. A multiplicity of perspectives provided by individuals from different cultural backgrounds can potentially illuminate blind spots related to assumptions and biases—allowing for a more nuanced understanding of potential pitfalls. Diversity in expertise will prove essential too; a team composed of engineers, social scientists, and ethicists is far better equipped to address the complexities of algorithmic bias than one consisting solely of software developers.

The second critical aspect of combating algorithmic discrimination involves continuous monitoring and evaluation. We must assess our AI systems throughout the development process and well into deployment—ensuring that undesirable biases are detected and addressed before they cause tangible harm. Organizations should embrace rigorous testing, validating their algorithms against key performance indicators to verify that the system is operating as intended. If biases are revealed through the process, programmers can revisit the data-source attributions, modify their models and retrain the system to decrease discriminatory outcomes.

In cases where biases within AI systems come to light only when deployed in real-world contexts—as exemplified by high-profile instances in criminal justice and employment screenings—it becomes crucial for stakeholders to engage in open dialogue and collaborate towards finding solutions. Transparent communication between technology companies, policymakers, affected communities, and civil society organizations will help bridge gaps in understanding, establish guidelines for rectifying errors within AI systems, and foster wider accountability.

By addressing biases in AI systems, we do not strive for perfection—a goal likely unattainable given the complexity of human behavior. Nevertheless, we aim to devise algorithms whose outputs mirror our collective aspirations for fairness and equity rather than perpetuating past biases.

Beyond facial recognition technology, the challenges surrounding algorithmic bias take on various forms across disciplines: biased sentence autocomplete suggestions due to skewed language data; biased risk assessment tools predicting an individual's likelihood of becoming a repeat offender; even biased web search results that perpetuate gender or racial stereotypes.

As we herald the potential of AI to address cognitive biases and aid in truth-seeking, another challenge that comes into focus is maintaining a delicate balance between the need to collect and analyze large swathes of data for decision-making and the responsibility to protect people's privacy. Much of the power in AI systems stems from their capacity to tap into vast amounts of information, discern patterns, and make informed predictions. However, this capability also raises valid concerns about breaches of privacy and potential misuse of personal information.

The revelations about Cambridge Analytica's data mining operations, which improperly collected private information about tens of millions of Facebook users without their consent, brought these issues to the forefront. While this particular instance did not involve AI decision-making per se, it highlights the ethical complexities that abound when personal data is treated as merely a means to some predetermined end.

So how do we nurture harmony between privacy rights and knowledge-sharing? A key strategy moving forward must entail developing ethical guidelines that govern the way organizations gather, store, process, and analyze data - especially with regard to sensitive personal information.

One framework that offers promising insights is that of "Privacy by Design," an approach that proactively integrates privacy considerations into every step of product development process. By ensuring that privacy is weaved into the very fabric of technologies from their inception—rather than being treated as an afterthought—we minimize risks associated with unauthorized access or misuse.

Moreover, technologies such as differential privacy can help strike the right balance between sharing valuable aggregated data insights while still preserving individual anonymity. Differential privacy provides a statistical framework for releasing "sanitized" information about a dataset while ensuring that sensitive details cannot be intercepted by malicious actors—even if they possess other pertinent background knowledge.

Another concept worth exploring is that of "data trusts," collaborative governance structures where groups constituted by individuals or organizations pool resources together in a bid to securely share data while simultaneously complying with regulatory requirements. Data trusts not only serve as custodians of sensitive information, but also foster transparency in the decision-making processes concerning data usage rights, privacy safeguards, and equitable sharing of the accruing benefits.

Gaining public trust must be the cornerstone for any organization aiming to operate ethically in the AI-driven landscape. To this end, it becomes imperative to institute robust mechanisms for handling user consent, data access rights, and the rectification or erasure of inaccurate or outdated data. Furthermore, ethical use policies should be formulated with input from a wide array of stakeholders—from end users and regulators to ethicists and technologists—offering a multidimensional understanding of privacy implications.

Respecting privacy alone is not enough; our quest for intellectual humility also necessitates fostering knowledge-sharing across disciplinary domains. The ability to access relevant datasets and resources from various fields can empower AI systems to break newfound ground by synthesizing insights hitherto unexplored.

Collaborative open science initiatives are instrumental in connecting scholars scattered across geographical borders but united in their pursuit of knowledge. For instance, CERN's Open Data Portal grants researchers access to data from particle physics experiments while preserving essential information about consent, publication policies, and guidelines on data reuse.

Furthermore, fostering closer interactions between academia and industry can only serve to enrich our understanding of the real-world implications of AI systems. Such collaborations have the potential to promote responsible knowledge-sharing practices while advancing both theoretical models and their practical applications.

In addressing the ethical complexities and challenges posed by AI-driven technologies, another pressing issue emerges—how do we demarcate and balance responsibility between the artificial agents making recommendations or predictions, and the human operators overseeing their actions?

Indeed, blind reliance on machines can inadvertently lead us into what is now recognized as "automation bias." Entrusting our decisions to AI systems can lull us into complacency and make us susceptible to errors. A study published in the Journal of Experimental Psychology revealed that participants who were provided with an algorithm's decision aid were more accepting of the AI's recommendation even when it was ostensibly mistaken. This phenomenon suggests that the allure of technology may embolden our willingness to defer to it—even when it shouldn't be trusted.

Another dimension worth considering pertains to moral responsibility. If an AI system makes a recommendation that later proves harmful, who should bear the brunt of the blame? The designers of the algorithm, program engineers, or perhaps those who implemented or abided by its decision?

Finding a way to properly distribute responsibility will be vital as we aim to leverage AI systems for enhancing human decision-making while preserving—and cherishing—our true capacity for intellectual humility. Central to this endeavor will be cultivating a deeper understanding of how responsibilities differ based on the degree and nature of human involvement, as well as variations in AI functionalities.

To illustrate this point more vividly, consider a framework proposed by philosopher Nancy Leveson in her analysis of safety-critical systems. She suggests viewing interactions between human operators and complex digital systems through three distinct lenses: Direct Responsibilities (DR), Indirect Responsibilities (IR), and Shared System Responsibilities (SSR).

In cases where humans retain direct control over decision-making with only superficial assistance from AI—primarily involving information pro-vision—the bulk of direct responsibilities fall on them. For instance, physicians who maintain control over diagnoses with an assistive AI guidance tool must shoulder most of the onus should something go awry.

As AI systems become more advanced and assume greater control over decision-making, responsibility begins to shift in complexity. Human collaborators now take on indirect responsibilities, such as overseeing the design, development, monitoring, and maintenance of the AI agents, while the artificial systems themselves shoulder some direct responsibilities.

In shared system responsibility scenarios, a complex web of accountability envelops both human and machine actors—each is indispensable to the collaborative process. Here, responsibilities are intertwined; neither human operators nor artificial agents can be seen as solely responsible for outcomes.

Although this framework provides an outline for pondering ways to assign responsibility in the context of human-AI partnerships, some questions continue to linger. For instance, how do we hold AI systems themselves accountable when they influence decisions in nuanced or hard-to-detect ways? Additionally, where does legal liability fall when there is no clear-cut path amidst the intricate interplay between humans and machines?

The allocation of responsibility must be both dynamic and contextual—taking into account an array of factors such as the level of human-AI collaboration, aspects of task delegation and goal direction, as well as regulatory norms. Furthermore, configuring boundaries of control between humans and machines demands continuous scrutiny and reflection upon the benefits versus potential pitfalls that accompany shifts in power distribution.

To strike this delicate balance between human operators and artificial agents effectively, organizations must invest in education initiatives designed to enhance understanding about AI capacities and limitations among their personnel. This empowers individuals to interact with machines in a responsible manner—appreciating when it's appropriate to defer to them while also maintaining a healthy skepticism of their recommendations.

35

Cultivating intellectual humility

Cultivating intellectual humility in an AI-driven world will require a cultural shift—one that gives precedence to curiosity-driven learning and encourages life-long education. This metamorphosis must be powered by technology, as it promises not only to deliver learning opportunities at unprecedented scales but also provides flexible and personalized adaptability catering to the needs of diverse learners. Our reliance on AI should not simply rest on utilizing machines to make decisions; we should also harness their proficiency in cultivating our minds and abilities.

Online learning platforms, from simple video tutorials to massive open online courses (MOOCs), have already begun transforming how people around the world access education. These resources democratize knowledge, challenging the traditional barriers of geography, socio-economic status, and even age or physical ability. Dispersing globally influential thought leaders' ideas within digital spaces, these platforms foster an environment connecting learners from disparate backgrounds—an integral component of intellectual humility.

As AI continues to advance, its potential to further enhance and personalize learning experiences grows increasingly palpable. For example, intelligent tutoring systems (ITS) are capable of simulating one-on-one interactions between students and human tutors. These AI-driven platforms adapt in real-time to users' varying needs—offering customized feedback, steering discussion in specific directions based on detected knowledge gaps, and adjusting content delivery according to individuals' learning styles.

Such personalized approaches help nurture the development of creativity and critical thinking skills—two essential tools at the core of intellectual humility. By refining one's ability to construct logically sound arguments, synthesize multifaceted information, and tackle complex challenges head-on, learners are better equipped to grapple with nuance, embrace shifting perspectives and appreciate the limits of their own understanding.

But empowering life-long learning goes beyond providing access to new educational technologies. We must reconceptualize our collective cultural values—embracing a society that genuinely prizes curiosity and accepts vulnerability when acknowledging our intellectual shortcomings.

One exemplar who embodies this spirit of intellectual humility and curiosity-driven learning is Benjamin Franklin. As a writer, entrepreneur, scientist, and statesman, Franklin was never confined by traditional disciplinary boundaries. He actively sought out new areas of inquiry, mastering fields as disparate as physics and diplomacy with remarkable aplomb.

In his autobiography, Franklin reflects on his pursuit of what he calls "moral perfection." Utilizing a minimalist notebook to chart his progress across thirteen different virtues—ranging from temperance to humility—Franklin endeavored to lead a life conducive to perpetual improvement.

Although he admits that his quest for moral perfection proved elusive—forever remaining an aspirational ideal—it's important to recognize the distinction between aiming for perfection and striving for continuous growth.

The latter sentiment captures a mindset keenly attuned to the value of life-long learning—one we must aspire to espouse in the age of AI-enhanced education.

To foster such values on a societal level, underlying educational infrastructure must also adapt. Traditional learning institutions must revisit their curricula, embracing interdisciplinary collaboration, promoting hands-on experiences and problem-solving activities that challenge students with real-world issues. Reforming our approaches to education not only bolsters academic performance but also actively cultivates the principles of intellectual humility.

Additionally, fostering collaboration between educational organizations and AI developers can drive more robust relationships between technology and education practices—an extension that symbiotically advances those fields while benefiting humanity at large.

Breaking down barriers impeding access to knowledge sources becomes increasingly crucial when realizing an AI-augmented world where intellectual humility thrives. We ought to be particularly mindful of empowering learners across all social strata—fostering networks that connect learners from diverse demographic backgrounds, fostering relationships enabling them to share ideas productively, challenge assumptions and learn from one another's unique perspectives.

The landscape of learning is rapidly changing, and the advent of powerful AI assistants presents us with new opportunities to satisfy our innate curiosity. These digital helpers lend themselves as tools that drive individuals to explore unfamiliar terrains and navigate the vast expanse of human knowledge in increasingly personalized ways.

Imagine a world where Siri or Alexa doesn't just answer simple queries or schedule your appointments but becomes an intellectual companion, a tireless mentor designed to help you satiate your thirst for discovery. Conversing with your AI assistant, you can plunge into novel fields or deepen your understanding of long-held interests – all through the power of technology.

Think back to that time in childhood when you were brimming with questions: "Why do birds fly?" "How do rockets take off?" "What makes a rainbow?" The same sense of wonderment that propelled these inquiries can now be directed towards an ever-present tutor who continually evolves and expands its own knowledge as it guides you on a lifelong journey of curiosity-driven exploration.

These AI assistants break down barriers to learning, making it easy for users to engage in informal yet ongoing self-education outside the boundaries of traditional institutions. This thirst for learning can now be quenched anywhere—during a morning walk, while preparing dinner, or even in between work meetings. The ubiquity and accessibility afforded by AI-fueled companions serve to transform the pursuit of knowledge into an integral part of daily life.

Curiosity-driven exploration is not only about consuming knowledge; it also entails posing questions and pondering uncharted terrain. AI assistants that effectively endorse this investigative mindset must cultivate their user's critical thinking skills by presenting new ideas while simultaneously encouraging original thought. Engaging AI mentors ought to prod users into questioning assumptions, grappling with diverse perspectives, and formulating hypotheses—all traits crucial in fostering intellectual humility.

Take the humble podcast as an example—a format that has captivated millions worldwide by inviting them to explore myriad realms through audio storytelling. These episodic programs can transport listeners into the lives of meticulous detectives, serial inventors, or even ancient civilizations—all within a matter of minutes. AI-powered listening platforms, with the ability to analyze granular user preferences and engage in natural language conversations, can harness this captivating format to immerse users in tailored explorations empathetically.

Envision AI applications that not only recognize and recommend podcasts capturing your fascination but also engage you in post-listening dialogue—inviting inquiries, reconciling conundrums, and furnishing cross-disciplinary connections that further stimulate your desire to explore a topic. In this scenario, an AI assistant is no longer just a curator of knowledge—it has transformed into an adept commentator, instigating dialogue and nurturing reflection, thus fostering life-long curiosity-driven exploration.

For both learners and mentors alike, curiosity often thrives when faced with challenges. Consider Garry Kasparov's legendary encounter with IBM's Deep Blue chess computer   a contest where man fought machine in a high-stakes duel of wits. Although Kasparov emerged defeated from that showdown, his tussle served as a catalyst for critical reflection and self-improvement.

Fast forward more than two decades later, and we find that AI-powered chess programs such as AlphaZero have revolutionized the game's strategy—completely upending long-established principles taught by grandmasters past. It is compelling evidence that even machines endowed with unparalleled intellect can act as an impetus for transformative human learning.

AI and machine learning algorithms are valuable tools not only for algorithmic prowess; they serve as catalysts beckoning us to tread unfamiliar pathways and expand our own intellectual horizons. By engaging with these AI mentors—posing puzzles that excite and unsettle our preconceptions—we expose ourselves to novel perspectives capable of inciting change in how we perceive the world around us.

Picture Pólya's famous book "How to Solve It" – a guide revered for teaching generations of mathematicians the beauty of problem-solving –

reincarnated as an AI tool imbued with human-like conversational aptitude. The combination of Pólya's innovative framework and AI's boundless computational potential could inspire countless individuals to uncover their innate mathematical talents, elevating the human spirit for exploration and creativity.

Now, let's think even bigger. The potential for AI-enhanced decision-making in reshaping the world's democratic landscape is undeniably vast. It can streamline bureaucratic processes, promote transparency, and facilitate robust communication between elected officials and their constituents. However, guarding against the perils of over-dependence on AI systems and preserving essential human values that animate democratic societies should remain at the forefront of our minds as we embrace this transformative technology.

Across time and cultures, robust democracies have cherished an intricate balance of power, ensuring that no single entity can wield excessive control. The allure of AI-enhanced decision-making comes with its own set of challenges—namely the temptation to yield human authority to machines that promise efficiency and data-driven accuracy. In these moments, it's crucial to remember that the essence of democracy lies not only in technocratic precision but also in fostering a culture that celebrates human deliberation and freedom of expression.

Safeguarding democratic norms while reaping the benefits of AI ultimately hinges upon cultivating a vigilant citizenry. Knowledgeable citizens capable of distinguishing AI's strengths and limitations will remain better equipped to participate meaningfully in public discourse vis-a-vis these technologies while holding governing bodies accountable for responsible implementation.

Consider, for instance, the burgeoning field of predictive policing—a domain where AI algorithms find patterns through mining vast amounts of data to forecast potential criminal behavior. While undoubtedly advantageous from a public safety standpoint, concerns arise regarding privacy infringement as well as biased outputs emanating from tainted inputs. Engaged communities, well-versed in AI's underlying mechanics, would help prop up mechanisms demanding accountability, staving off potential misuse and ensuring that democratic principles remain insulated from infringement.

Moreover, proactive efforts around policy formulation will be instrumental in safeguarding these lofty ideals. Laws designed with foresight—juxtaposing AI-enhanced efficiency gains with priorities like fairness and privacy protection—can strike a robust equilibrium between man and machine in the realm of democracy. Thought leaders and policymakers should deeply engage with multidisciplinary experts, encompassing fields such as data ethics, human rights, and computer science, fostering a collaborative approach towards policy creation.

There is also the growing challenge of disinformation or so-called "deepfake" technology. This AI-generated deception has stoked fears about undermining trust in democratic institutions and endangering the very fabric of truth—the cornerstone upon which democratic decision-making resides. To mitigate these risks, investing in public awareness campaigns aiming to educate communities about discerning accurate information from falsehoods must become an urgent priority.

AI-driven fact-checking initiatives can greatly enhance this process—leveraging machine learning algorithms to run vast quantities of information through falsifiability gauntlets. By incorporating AI-driven tools to verify news sources and expose deepfakes for what they are, we can empower citizens to stay vigilant against these new-age threats without curtailing access to robust and diverse perspectives.

Similarly, as AI takes its place within governance structures' inner workings—promising optimized resource allocation and policymaker accountability—it should never fully supplant essential human decision-making components. A healthy democracy thrives on lively debate where individuals thoughtfully consider multiple facets of a given issue before reaching consensus through discussions steeped in empathy and mutual respect.

AI systems can be employed as advisers or consultants synthesizing myriad viewpoints while complementing human contemplation—the result, a harmonious interplay between computational prowess and human ingenuity nourishing collective wisdom.

An exemplary case lies in envisioning a modern-day House of Commons where members periodically consult personalized AI intuitions that analyze constituent feedback from varied networks. These streams could include social media feeds, opinion surveys, or town hall engagements collating inputs that capture public sentiment around pressing issues. Members then bring these insights back into the Parliament's chamber as they cross swords with opposing views—all while being cognizant of their AI advisement's intrinsic worth and limitations.

Ultimately, striking an equilibrium between AI's merits and preserving democratic norms will turn on cultivating environments wherein artificial intelligence and human intuition coalesce, mutually reinforcing and refining each other. This synergistic union creates the building blocks for robust, well-informed systems shaped by empathetic deliberation—system characteristics that are quintessentially democratic.

One of the key elements in a democracy is consensus-building—the dialogue that forms the very bedrock of political decision-making. From this perspective, AI can be thought of as a powerful tool for facilitating dialogue between communities with differing opinions or entrenched beliefs.

Imagine an AI-mediated platform that enables communication across political or ideological divides—an environment where debaters converse openly devoid of hostility or rancor. Not only could this foster mutual understanding in the short term, but it could also foster empathy among those who may have otherwise remained disconnected from one another.

257

36

Towards a more enlightened future

Imagine an idyllic future in which our cognitive biases retreat into the shadows as artificial intelligence emerges to champion creativity, bridging age-old divides and unshackling the human spirit. As machines extend their tentacles—unraveling the blindfolds that have held sway over our intellectual horizons—the boundaries of the possible give way to a cornucopia of outlandish prospects. We stand on the cusp of a realm bristling with boundless creative potential, one that is ripe for exploration.

This not-so-distant world prompts us to reconsider our understanding of creativity as we witness awe-inspiring innovations propelled by the power of AI. No longer strictly the purview of humans, creativity becomes a force melding together the ingenuity of both man and machine.

Take, for example, an artist standing before her 21st-century canvas, poised to capture nature's resplendent effervescence in bold brushstrokes. Suddenly, she hesitates as her AI-enabled paintbrush offers alternate hues and techniques that might better render her vision—together they unleash a veritable revelation reimagining art's long-standing paradigms—an enthralling dance between human sentiment and technological precision.

This new era of emancipated creativity brings forth hitherto unconceivable collaborations between humans and AI that are capable of yielding extraordinary results. Let us examine architecture—a field predicated upon balancing aesthetic flair with functional acuity. Traditional design constraints dissolving under this fresh perspective's compelling gaze make way for ground-breaking architectural masterpieces encapsulating AI-derived principles such as biomimicry.

By incorporating these organic structures where human whimsy encounters engineered precision, we sow the seeds for a built environment steeped in harmony with its ecological milieu—one fostering vivacious communities espousing core tenets of sustainability. Here too, we witness machines offer invaluable insight by simulating countless permutations with unprecedented speed and informing design choices—further pushing creative boundaries.

Similarly, the world of fashion witnesses the melding of human intuition with AI-augmented styling prowess. Traditionally, designers reigned supreme as the ultimate purveyors of style—defining each season's sartorial zeitgeist. This enduring reality now finds itself amidst a virtuosic paradigm shift that seeks to democratize fashion, enabling it to morph into a more fluid, personalized domain. Emerging from this metamorphosis is a distinctive synthesis: Human creativity abetted by machine learning algorithms that produce entirely unique garments tailor-made for individualistic tastes.

Indeed, we observe an exhilarating vista unfolding before our eyes—a future where augmented human creativity partnered up with AI-driven decision-making paves the way for a tangible cultural renaissance. The zenith of artistry lies not beyond our imaginative grasp but instead materializes within it the moment our intellect becomes unshackled and unfettered—a radical transformation made possible by artificial intelligence.

In such a liberated creative landscape, each individual can take ownership of their creative destinies—availing themselves to tools once reserved solely for elite practitioners in fields like cinematography or music production. AI ushers in this new age where creativity flourishes on an unprecedented scale.

Picture a young aspiring musician who couldn't have dreamt of matching her compositions with expertly produced accompaniments until she encountered her AI-enabled virtual orchestra. An inexhaustible reserve of sonic possibilities lying at her fingertips allows her to fine-tune opulent melodies in homage to both cherished classics and bold avant-garde idiosyncrasies—a reverie emblematic of this rich future of emancipated creativity. Despite potential limitations, this new wave of creativity will likely come with complex discussions around ethical issues, such as intellectual property rights or determining the original creators in an ever-changing landscape.

Beyond the traditional realm of artistic expression lies a world where AI-augmented creativity breathes life into unforeseen opportunities for human endeavors and personal growth. Imagine embarking on an odyssey underpinned by our pursuit of cognitive unshackling, a journey that transcends limitations and elevates the essence of what it means to be human.

Envision an age where artificial intelligence dispels occupational drudgery, allowing individuals to embrace their passions, delve into novel domains, and carve out distinctive avenues of self-expression long stifled by the societal dictates of subsistence. No mere idle reverie, this transformative vision reflects an inspiring trajectory already set in motion.

By minimizing manual labor's necessity and automating repetitive tasks, AI endows humans with the freedom to cultivate nuanced skills and untapped talents nestled within their cores. This unbridled exploration paves new paths for personal growth—eschewing dogmatic adherence in favor of resounding self-actualization.

We can picture a harbor bustling with ships transporting divers and marine biologists projecting 3D maps generated by AI-enhanced data sets to explore the ocean depths. These experts collaborate across disciplines and cultures to unravel the marine ecosystem's intricate tapestry, harnessing AI's precision analytical abilities to establish sustainable interaction between society and its aquatic frontier.

Such collaborative ventures open doors to numerous possibilities that transcend disciplinary boundaries—bringing together specialists from disparate realms like ecology, chemistry, anthropology, and statistics. A glance at scientific research's blossoming landscape reveals thriving alliances enabled by artificial intelligence overcoming cognitive barriers once impregnable to disjointed human endeavor.

As these innovative hubs abound, we discover nurturing ecosystems wherein scholarly pursuit thrives in symbiosis with practical execution—a veritable playground for all who dare push boundaries and defy convention. As meticulous analysis interweaves with the joyous embrace of curiosity, these intellectual crucibles foster groundbreaking achievements while nurturing minds enriched by both trial and tribulation.

Moreover, the novel terrain that emerges when human-centric vocations meld with AI-augmented innovations elicits the need for an evolving skillset which galvanizes a continuous learning mindset. This overarching paradigm fosters resilience strengthened by adaptability—crystallizing into a future focused on acquiring knowledge and developing competencies.

Injecting the power of AI into the personal development sphere, such educational endeavors offer unbounded gateways nurturing both career advancement and personal enhancement. Comprehensive online courses tailored to individuals' learning styles and resource availability fan the flames of lifelong learning, fueled by AI-driven engines devoted to combating biases and engendering intellectual humility.

Imagine a person seeking a drastic career change after years within one field—a numerical analyst trading in spreadsheets for observing wildlife. Artificial intelligence, as their trusty accomplice, deftly assesses pertinent gaps in their knowledge, fashioning customized courses targeting specific areas of growth. With this newfound mastery comes transformative opportunity buttressed by machines working tirelessly to ensure success.

In turn, these tools fashioned by artificial intelligence shape not only our tangible expertise but also our internal landscapes. The mindful embrace of AI-enhanced meditation apps underscores the quest for mental serenity within an era of rapid disruption. Utilizing data derived from wearable devices offering biofeedback alongside customized guidance on emotional regulation exercises attests to AI's significance in fostering holistic growth.

Innovative virtual therapy integration with machine learning algorithms opens new doors where professionals, in tandem with their mechanized counterparts, work intimately to combat mental afflictions plaguing millions. This invaluable contribution chips away at societal stigma surrounding mental health while rendering therapy accessible to those who may have lacked adequate support systems before this transformation.

The thriving intersection of human creativity and advanced technology bodes well for prospering communities—conjuring visions of flourishing neighborhoods pulsating with vibrant energy. When citizens are encouraged to forge research collectives or embark upon grassroots campaigns aimed at addressing the pressing needs of both the environment and their peers, AI emerges as a steadfast ally in this virtuous struggle. Such conscientious efforts reverberate throughout society—catalyzing collective progress where minds meld with AI-driven tools in the pursuit of equitable solutions to shared challenges.

We stand on the precipice of a world brimming with AI-augmented potential, eager to conquer cognitive barriers and create harmonious synergies. The stage is set for a global community to flourish where truth-seeking, intellectual humility, and a collaborative spirit underpin collective action. Envision humanity embracing AI as a trustworthy companion endeavoring to advance the common good.

By dispelling the shroud of entrenched falsehoods, AI steers humanity towards harnessing truth within various realms—be it our natural environment, social structures, or personal experiences. The constant pursuit of truth demands that we shine a spotlight on our biases and fallacies—those insidious snags that trap us within the quagmire of ignorance. When artificial intelligence ventures boldly into such uncharted territories, it unravels previously overlooked perspectives while piloting our search for answers where once confusion reigned.

This burgeoning relationship between humans and machines instills valuable lessons in intellectual humility—an attribute akin to a compass guiding our search for truth while safeguarding against overconfidence's perils. Suppose you find yourself at odds with long-standing beliefs challenged by fresh insights garnered through AI-driven explorations. In that case, the ability to admit fallibility paves the way for healthier discourse where intractable positions yield to reasonable accommodation.

Welcome to the age where a diverse cadre of scientists, craftsmen, policymakers, and educators congregates around AI-assisted platforms—transcending geographical barriers to pursue shared objectives like climate change mitigation or equal education opportunities. Picture this spirited confluence as streams converging into rivers where invaluable knowledge flows uninhibited across domains and geographies.

This newfound fluidity dissolved entrenched barriers previously insurmountable due to linguistic limitations fostering miscommunication—a significant hindrance when envisioning solutions demanded by urgent global predicaments. AI-driven language translation systems bridge these divides empowering inclusive dialogue where individuals partake in novel collaborations unfettered by the bounds of mother tongues.

In turn, AI engenders empathy, a capacity vital when fostering cultural understanding or navigating clashing perspectives — essential ingredients to achieve durable consensus. Such machine-augmented systems prove particularly potent when seeking common ground across wide-ranging audiences—capturing nuances often misinterpreted or lost in tradition-driven translation.

Imagine convening a town hall with citizens from diverse backgrounds and employing AI tools that disentangle the crux of participants' convictions on pressing civic issues. These toolkits masterfully condense vital elements of discourse, laying bare the fundamental passions and anxieties fueling citizens' opinions. This distilled essence simplifies the labyrinthine task of drafting coordinated policy responses that respect competing viewpoints while surging forward to tackle societal challenges head-on.

The cultivation of a global community valuing harmony melds with AI's transformative capabilities within realms such as natural disaster management. Sophisticated algorithms rapidly detect harbingers of calamity and orchestrate swifter response tactics—minimizing casualties and amplifying the allocation of resources where needed most. Efficacious strategies emerge where policymakers worldwide heed vital warnings presented by machines acting as vigilant sentinels.

This artificial intelligence-powered web spins threads connecting distant communities willing to extend assistance to neighbors facing grave misfortune. Empathy blossoms as human compassion manifests in generous acts where fellow beings are galvanized into action by AI forecasts painting poignant portraits of possible calamities lacking any benign redresses.

Furthermore, institutions and governments can harness AI technologies in facilitating cooperation and unity across borders. As digitally integrated diplomacy gains traction, we witness swift resolutions to disputes and deadlocks that once seemed indomitable. Artificial intelligence amplifies discussions between nations with an acute focus on overarching goals—an unwavering compass training our sights on solutions rather than obstinate entrenchments.

Consider this peculiar paradox: Increased reliance on AI enhances the essence of humanity through novel methods that celebrate unity amidst diversity—an invigorating recalibration of our species' core strengths. The global community cultivates elements usually left unspoken, like respect and understanding, reinstating humanity's crucial role in a machine-dominated landscape.

This vision of a harmonious global community radiates glimpses of hope, pioneering a new epoch delineated by amity and unity. Here, the avid pursuit of truth blends seamlessly with the intellectual humility to forge bonds solidified by empathy—inspiring trust in artificial intelligence as a faithful ally that enhances the essence of being human.

Boundless opportunities beckon on the horizon where AI enriches personal growth, substantiates human endeavor, and propels communities to cherish values born from empathy. This landscape whispers tantalizing potential—an invitation to step forth towards uncharted terrain hand-in-hand with artificial intelligence. Through this arduous but exhilarating journey, we breathe life into a world where harmony, truth, and intellectual humility form foundations of our collective aspirations.